PROVENCE
gastronomique

PROVENCE
gastronomique

ERICA BROWN

FOREWORD BY MARIE-PIERRE MOINE

PHOTOGRAPHY BY DEBBIE PATTERSON

SERIES EDITOR MARIE-PIERRE MOINE

Conran Octopus

First published in Great Britain in 1995 by
Conran Octopus Limited
37 Shelton Street
London WC2H 9HN

British Library Cataloguing-in-Publication Data
A catalogue record for this book is available from
the British Library.

ISBN 1 85029 669 3

Senior Editor **SARAH PEARCE**
Editor **CHARLOTTE COLEMAN-SMITH**
Art Editor **KAREN BOWEN**
Text Editor **SARAH RIDDELL**
Recipe Editor **BEVERLY LE BLANC**
Production **MANO MYLVAGANAM**
Typesetting **LIZA BRUML**

Printed in Hong Kong

NOTE ON RECIPES Both metric and imperial quantities
are given. Use either all metric or all imperial, as the
two are not interchangeable.

CONTENTS

FOREWORD

I experienced my first taste of Provence at the age of six while staying on an island near Toulon. A new-found friend showed me how to bash the pinecones from the trees lining the alley behind the kitchen, in order to extract the sweetly nutty kernels. Later on that summer, I had leftover toast rubbed with garlic and spread with butter that was ever so slightly rancid, and a tiny sampling of sea urchin roe. All the while, there was the sound of cicadas chirping and unfamiliar voices ending each word on an upward lilt, as if with a smile. Then there was the sea; the scented wilderness of the *garrigue*; plump, creeping plants tantalizingly called *sorcières*, and a lighthouse that beamed in and out of my bedroom right through the night. The house had neither electricity nor running water. For me, this was thrilling stuff, but not quite paradise because the sun burnt, the sand was gritty and the seasalt stung. Nevertheless, I was hooked and have been ever since.

Erica Brown's **Provence Gastronomique** brings back the excitement of that first visit. Her enthusiasm is infectious, but she never lapses into sentimentality. With great perception, she vividly describes the contrasts and paradoxes of Provence and relates these to the region's cusine. She never forgets that what she calls the 'land of the languid lunch' is also a country where the soil is largely rocky and meagre, and where not so long ago people were prepared to fight to the death for access to water.

Although it may be frugal and resourceful, the cooking of Provence is never crude. Erica Brown's selection of recipes shows how it relies on herbs, olive oil and garlic to turn available ingredients into uniquely palatable dishes that are bursting with flavour. These dishes are more varied and also often much more subtle than you would expect from Mediterranean food. Over the centuries many of the recipes of Provence have been honed into classics – golden *aïoli*, melting daubes, fragrant roast lamb and grilled fish – all of which are amongst the best examples of country cooking. The book also captures the way in which, in the skilled hands of the current generation of innovative chefs, the gastronomy of Provence is paying tribute to its roots in a decidedly exciting post-nouvelle-cuisine way. The recipes for stuffed vegetables, in particular, had me rushing to my local market in a flurry of experimentation. There is more than enough in **Provence Gastronomique** to keep the reader in happy expectation until he or she can hear the cicadas chirping.

Marie-Pierre Moine

BELOW RIGHT The promenade des Anglais in Nice was a nineteenth-century make-work programme funded by English residents after the local orange harvest failed. Now France's fifth largest city, Nice, like most of the Riviera, presents a largely commercial face to visitors. But the narrow, winding streets of the old town still charm, and there is one of Provence's best daily markets in the Cours Saleya.

TOP ROW Much of Provence's traditional economy depended on the twin staples of olive oil and wine, both introduced by the Greeks in the sixth and fifth centuries B.C. The vines of Gigondas in the Vaucluse (left) produce a sturdy red wine which can compete with its neighbour, Châteauneuf-du-Pape (the best in Provence). Olive groves around Nice produce a fruity olive oil from the local le Cailletier variety (centre).
ABOVE AND TOP RIGHT Newer crops include strawberries and delicate courgette flowers now grown year-round under glass near Nice.

INTRODUCTION

The first time I went to Provence, it was June. I flew into Nice airport, stayed on the chic boulevard de la Croisette in Cannes, and made gastronomic forays into the nearby hills to eat under the Michelin stars. Days were spent exploring the warm sandy beaches and red-tiled hilltop villages aglow in the sun's bright reflections. This, I thought, was Provence; prosperous playground of the rich, sunny land of the languid lunch.

The next time I went to Provence, it was November. I travelled by train to Antibes and drove up the hillsides to the old *mas*, the farmhouse I'd rented near Grasse. The same Michelin stars still twinkled nearby but here I was feeding myself. Saturday mornings saw me back in Antibes for the market, amazed by the profusion – in winter! – of glistening multi-coloured fish; the freshest, greenest of vegetables; the softest, rosiest of fruit. The strangeness of seeing olives – green, amber, purple and black – bought loose from great tubs instead of packed into small jars, the hard slabs of salt cod and long skeins of garlic. What abundance! This, I thought, was Provence.

Every week I gave in to temptation and always overbought. By Monday my northern thrift would take hold and I'd spend a day being creative with leftovers, often watching for signs of any of the many winds that could so quickly, and that winter did, fan a flame into a forest fire, for by that time I had discovered that the *mas* was called *La Croix des Vents* (the four winds). This is a region that claims over thirty winds, led by the mighty *mistral*: its unpredictable and ferocious swirling brings clear blue skies along with it, but also biting cold and frayed tempers. It is true that I was in no real danger. Behind the house, all was scrub and rock and in front were the terraced rows of jasmine my landlord grew for the perfume industry in Grasse.

In January, he invited me to watch as he pulled a copper alembic out of a lean-to shed, lit a fire of vine prunings under it and made his own small quantity of *eau de vie*. His wife appeared, shaking the olives from the few gnarled trees around the house into plastic nets laid on the ground, picking up the overspill on her hands and knees and taking the harvest to the nearby mill to be pressed into oil to see her through the year.

She had pointed me to all the herbs I would ever need – rosemary, thyme, sage, the summer savory called *sarriette* which only grows in Provence – all of which were somehow thriving on the meagre soil between every rocky outcrop around the house. Her husband had introduced me to the '*cubi*', the five-litre plastic container that I took to the wine

ABOVE The definitive tastes of Provence are as
much about aromas as they are about flavours.
These include anisette *made from fennel seeds
and used to flavour* cachous *(tiny sweets),*
desserts and, of course, pastis, *the most
famous of local aperitifs.*

RIGHT ABOVE Vines grow throughout the Var to
make the increasingly highly regarded
Côtes de Provence wines.

RIGHT BELOW Lavender is grown not just for the
fragrance industry but also for culinary use to
infuse sauces, ice cream and as an essential
component of herbes de Provence.

OPPOSITE ABOVE Picholine olives are one of many
varieties of this versatile fruit. Picked green in
October, they are often made into olives cassées;
the olives are split, steeped in water and then
brined with herbs and aromatics.

OPPOSITE BELOW October is also the month of the
almond harvest, especially in the Vaucluse
where the trees still flourish.

co-operative down the road to be filled with the local rosé for a few francs. I learned, like them, to finish my Saturday shopping and sit over a *pastis* in a nearby café watching the world go by until the market closed at lunchtime. Then we would load up our car boots with empty wooden fruit boxes, salvaged from the market, to use as free kindling for the fire you needed to see you through the cold, Provençal nights.

As I slowly got to know them, they allowed me to take the occasional lemon from the one tree that grew in their garden and a few times we invited each other round for an evening drink. I quickly learned that little dishes of olives, almonds and radishes, or plates of sliced baguette spread with home-made *tapenade* or *anchoïade* were obligatory accompaniments to any aperitif.

From these lessons in self-sufficiency, I realized that I had experienced something of the real Provence, the apparent romance and glamour only thinly disguising a harsh land whose inhabitants had, for centuries, eked out a hard life from few natural resources and where nothing ever was allowed to go to waste. A land, too, much fought over since at least the sixth century B.C. and isolated from the rest of France until just over a century ago, when the advent of the railways meant that Provence was united with the markets and peoples of the north.

FIRST SETTLERS

The coastline of Provence was first colonized by Greeks known as Phoceans, who founded the port of Marseille around 600 B.C. and those of Antibes (Antipolis) and Nice, a century or so later. Basically maritime traders, they also introduced the olive and the vine to the region, the traditional – and still important – bases of the Provençal economy. But it was the Roman settlers who first gave it the name *Provincia*: the first Roman province and a place where officers of Caesar's legions who had served there and built great cities such as Arles, Nîmes and Orange chose, like many after them, to retire.

The Romans retreated with their Empire around A.D. 500, leaving Provence at the mercy of waves of invaders for most of the next five hundred years. Franks, Saracens, Vikings and Magyars all took their turn to terrorize the land. In the eighth century A.D., peace reigned briefly under Charlemagne, but local wars and religious persecution continued almost until the French Revolution.

Well into this century, most Provençaux could best be described as hunter-gatherers even when, if they were lucky, they kept a 'poor man's cow' (a goat) for milk and cheese, a hive of bees for honey and cultivated a few vines and a fig tree or two. They caught fish from rivers and sea; shot feathered and furred game on plateaux and hills; gathered olives, almonds, walnuts, mushrooms, truffles, herbs and fruit growing wild. Summer fruit and vegetables were preserved in honey syrup or olive oil for winter. Beans, grapes and plums were dried, fish was salted. Shepherds tended small flocks on the high rocky plateaux called *garrigues*, living with their beasts and moving up to the high Alps each summer for the annual migration.

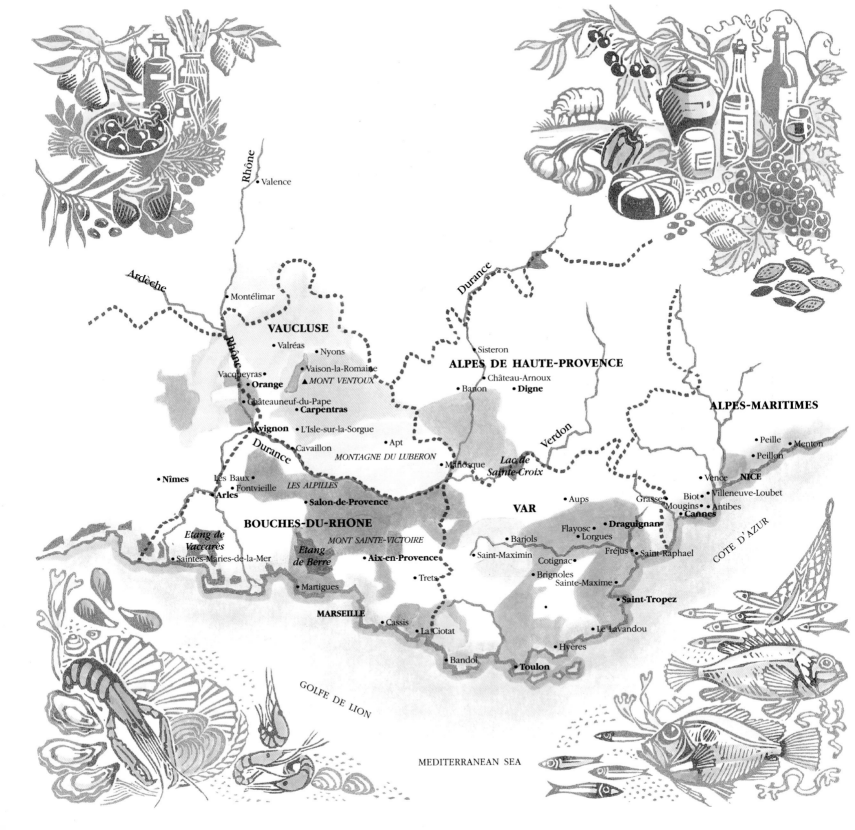

Rhône

• Valence

Ardèche

• Montélimar

Rhône

VAUCLUSE

• Valréas   • Nyons

Vacqueyras •   Vaison-la-Romaine •
Orange   ▲ *MONT VENTOUX*

• Châteauneuf-du-Pape
                Carpentras

Avignon •   • L'Isle-sur-la-Sorgue

Durance   • Cavaillon   • Apt

Nîmes •   *MONTAGNE DU LUBERON*
        Les Baux •
        • Fontvieille   *LES ALPILLES*
Arles •
                        Salon-de-Provence

BOUCHES-DU-RHONE
                MONT SAINTE-VICTOIRE
Etang de
Vaccarès   *Etang*
                de Berre   **Aix-en-Provence** •
• Saintes-Maries-de-la-Mer
                                • Trets
                • Martigues

MARSEILLE
                • Cassis
                        • La Ciotat
                • Bandol
                        Toulon

GOLFE DE LION

Durance

• Sisteron

ALPES DE HAUTE-PROVENCE

• Château-Arnoux
• Banon   **Digne**

Verdon

• Manosque   *Lac de*
                Sainte-Croix

VAR
                        • Aups
                        Flayosc •   **Draguignan**
        • Barjols   • Lorgues
• Saint-Maximin   Fréjus •
        Cotignac •   • Saint-Raphael
        • Brignoles
        Sainte-Maxime •
                        Saint-Tropez
                •
                        • Le Lavandou
                • Hyères

ALPES-MARITIMES

                • Peille   • Menton
                        • Peillon
        • Vence   **NICE**
Grasse •   Biot • Villeneuve-Loubet
        Mougins •   • Antibes
                Cannes
                        COTE D'AZUR

MEDITERRANEAN SEA

GLORIOUS ISOLATION

WINE REGIONS

Coteaux du Tricastin

Côtes du Rhône

Châteauneuf-du-Pape

Côtes du Rhône Villages

Côtes du Ventoux

Tavel

Lirac

Palette

Gigondas

Beaumes-de-Venise

Coteaux du Lubéron

Coteaux d'Aix-en-Provence

Coteaux Varois

Cassis

Bandol

Coteaux de Pierrevert

Côtes de Provence

Bellet

A glance at a map explains it all. To the north, Provence was geographically cut off from the rest of France by mountain ranges pierced by few passes. Those there were proved difficult to cross. Apart from the coastal strip along the Mediterranean and the wide Rhône delta, the land rises and falls in a series of dramatic upheavals on its way to the sea, creating convoluted mountain ranges. The only stretches of flat land are the *garrigues*, and they can only support scrub. Valleys and, therefore, fertile pastures are few and narrow. Rivers, fed from undergound springs, are raging torrents in winter and early spring, mere trickles amid the dust and stones of their beds in summer and autumn.

The lack of pastures means no cows, which in turn means no beef or dairy produce. Sheep and goats were kept for milk and cheese, not for their meat, while chickens were more valuable for their eggs than for their flesh. Of course, at the end of their productive life, the livestock was slaughtered, but only to produce tough, stringy meat. Hence the ubiquitous daube: a stew most often of mutton with olive oil, wine, herbs, and the essential piece of orange peel, left all day in its covered dish to cook itself slowly into tenderness. For fresh meat, families depended on whatever game could be trapped or shot for the pot, but well into this century most families tasted meat only once a week if they were lucky. It is easy to see why the traditional Easter *gigot* (roasted leg of lamb) or roast *cabri* (kid) is still regarded as a great family feast.

The Mediterranean, of course, provided fresh fish but again, until recently, only to fishermen and their neighbours. The coastal hills rise steeply, sometimes straight from the sea itself, creating enclosed fishing communities clustered around small harbours. Transporting fish any distance was impossible unless it was salted or otherwise preserved. Valleys, where rivers dried up for months of the year, could grow wheat and vegetables although the fierce heat of summer and the short, but sometimes very sharp, winters meant that production was limited.

Luckily, the olive and the vine liked the land and the climate, and salt was provided naturally in the vast salt pans in the Camargue at the mouth of the Rhône. The importance of these natural resources could not be overestimated and not just for their dietary value. Olive oil and wine preserved fruit and vegetables for winter, while salt preserved fish to take protein to the population inland. But most important, they were staples of trade.

From the earliest days Provence traded with the other nations of the Mediterranean rather than the rest of France. Trading olive oil, wines and salt with north Africa brought Arab flavours (like cinnamon and raisins) into traditional dishes. The more recent influx of emigrants from Algeria has reinforced their influence, especially around Marseille (which has its own Arab market) and Arles. Italian influences obviously go back to the Romans but Nice and its hinterland were part of Italy until 1860 and, even then, their inhabitants were fond of pasta, polenta and *pistou* (Genoese pesto). Pizza is now found everywhere. Spain supplied red peppers, tomatoes and paella, and even Scandinavia played a part: Viking fishermen traded dried and salt cod for olive oil (the latter two combine in *brandade de morue*, one of the most traditional of Provençal dishes, see page 84).

THRIFT IN ABUNDANCE

All traditional dishes were designed to avoid waste. Small amounts of meat were made to last by making *farcis* (vegetables scooped out and stuffed with a mixture of their flesh, rice or breadcrumbs and chopped meat, all bound with olive oil). The vegetable *tian*, as traditional as the daube, would have carefully hoarded shreds of leftover meat tucked into it before being cooked and gratinéed. Shards of crystallized or candied fruit would be chopped into the traditional Christmas bread known as *pompe*, or *fougasse*. Leftover crumbs of goats' or sheep's cheese would be kneaded with a 'mother' of blue cheese, pepper and fiery *eau de vie* to ferment into *lou cachat*, a pungent spread. Even the now-fashionable 'designer' salad known as *mesclun*, these days grown from purposely mixed seeds of various leaves and herbs, originated as a way of using vegetable thinnings.

So for economic reasons, Provence is the only part of France where herbs, fruit and vegetables have traditionally provided the core of the cuisine. Aubergines, courgettes, artichokes, peppers, onions, garlic and, more recently, tomatoes, have always thrived in the long sunny days. Lemons, oranges and other citrus fruits have always grown along the Mediterranean coast as it nears the Italian border. Almonds, peaches, apricots and cherries make the Rhône valley and the hillsides of Vaucluse a mass of pale blossoms in the spring. In the past, every smallholder grew what greens he could. Herbs – lavender, rosemary, thyme, sage, bay and *sarriette* – were gathered from scrubby hillsides, their fragrance made especially intense by the summer heat, to infuse every dish with their flavours. But the remoteness of Provence from the rest of France combined with the long, hot, dry summers ensured that in most years little more than self-sufficiency was achieved.

It was the coming of the railway in the 1860s that transformed the Provençal economy. Suddenly the whole area was accessible. This not only heralded the advent of tourism from the north but also, for the first time, offered a speedy form of transport that could deliver southern fruit and vegetables to the northern markets still fresh. It became economic to irrigate thousands of hectares of land to grow all kinds of fruit and vegetables much earlier than anywhere else in France and to send them to Paris to be sold *en primeur* where they would command premium prices. These twin factors – tourists in, produce out – rapidly increased in importance as transport became even faster after the Second World War, and they are now the mainstays of Provence's economy.

Today, the Bouches-du-Rhône is one great market garden – and Provence as a whole supplies the tables of northern Europe with a succession of fruits and vegetables year round. Now, the larger markets such as those at Arles, Aix, Nice and Cannes overflow with seasonal abundance: cabbages, leeks, pumpkins, thistle-like cardoons, a cornucopia of wild and cultivated mushrooms, artichokes, clementines, apples and pears from autumn to early spring. There are asparagus, spinach, beans, peas, salad leaves running the gamut of shades of green; courgette flowers, cherries, apricots, melons, peaches, strawberries through spring and summer, and onions, garlic, parsley, aubergines, tomatoes and artichokes, almost all year round. Imported fruit and vegetables now blur the seasons but for those who wish to eat local produce seasonally, there is no lack of variety.

ABOVE Provençal cuisine could not exist without the herbs which flourish everywhere under the hot sun – even in almost soil-free rocky crevices. Because almost everyone grows their own, they're rarely seen as cut bunches in the markets or shops. However some of the larger markets, such as the Saturday one in Arles, sell a wide variety in pots. Favourites include basil, sage, chives, parsley and tarragon.

RIGHT Herbs are the answer to the self-caterer's prayers, as is the wide assortment of fresh fish available in Provence, such as red mullet, sea bass and John Dory. The varieties may be unfamiliar but none needs more than to be brushed with olive oil and grilled or barbecued, preferably over coals or wood given added fragrance by the addition of fresh fennel branches.

CORNERSTONES OF CUISINE

With all the choice available, the four cornerstones of Provençal cuisine still reign supreme: the olive and its oil, garlic and wild herbs, three ancient companions joined latterly by their youthful partner, the tomato. Olive oil has always been the universal cooking medium here, with different types pressed in four main centres: Nyons in the north, Mausanne in the south, Draguignan in central Provence, and Nice in the east. Garlic, whether white-skinned from the Vaucluse or pink-tinged from Bouches-du-Rhône, is an essential – though not necessarily obvious – component of almost every savoury dish. Together, they come to an apotheosis in *aïoli*, the garlic mayonnaise served everywhere (see page 34).

Herbs flavour everything, sometimes even without being added to a dish. Such is the case with the famous Sisteron lamb of Haute-Provence and its brother '*agneau du soleil*' in the Lubéron: the herbs on which they graze lend a subtle flavour to their meat. Tomatoes are now so ubiquitous that *à la Provençale* has come to mean any dish containing them even though tomatoes only arrived in Provence a century or so ago (in fact, most 'traditional' Provençal dishes cannot be traced much further back than that). Before the vital lifeline of the railway, most people lived on vegetables and fruit, with protein in the form of meat, fish, or cheese only eaten as a rare treat.

Provençal cooking has the virtue of being fairly adaptable: many ingredients are interchangeable, depending on what's available in the market, and the amount of, say, garlic can be increased or decreased to suit your own taste. Almost all dishes have several, equally valid, versions. Most daube recipes will work with lamb or beef and most *tians* can easily be adapted for different vegetables. Vegetable *mélanges*, such as *ratatouille* (see page 35) or *soupe au pistou* (see page 121) can have their proportions varied. There is only one knack – but like most tricks of the trade, it's not that easy to learn: flavours are always intense but they are never heavy-handed. So far, so obvious, but the real sleight-of-hand is more subtle. The best Provençal cooks manage to make sure that no one taste stands out individually but that a dish is noticeably lessened if any element is left out. This is as much about aromas – of wine, garlic, citrus, herbs, even truffles – as about taste.

It is ironic that the traditional diet of the region, born as it was from poverty and paucity, should exemplify the healthy way we are now exhorted to eat. Indeed this is no fad, it *is* healthy. The medicinal qualities of garlic, olive oil and herbs, especially, have been well-known for centuries.

Today, not only are Provençal chefs starting to return to their traditional culinary roots, but all the ingredients needed to prepare Provençal recipes can be found in supermarkets all over the world. It is simplicity itself to combine them in the relaxed Provençal way, for most of the recipes are also adaptable when it comes to quantity, and even cooking time. I would encourage you to experiment, bearing in mind that the same ingredients will have different intensities of flavour depending on the season and that the one mantra to bear in mind is 'fresh, fresher, freshest'.

'*Faites simple*,' the famous dictum of the great chef, Auguste Escoffier, could have been coined for this food. Perhaps it was, for he was a son of Provence.

TOP Garlic is the universal perfume of Provence, whether used discreetly to give an underlying hint of itself, or robustly dominating a dish such as aïoli *(garlic mayonnaise). Purple/pink varieties from the Var and Bouches-du-Rhône are more gentle than the white variety grown in the Vaucluse. Sometimes garlic is used as whole heads, cut in half crossways and cooked slowly with a roast* gigot *(leg of lamb) or* cabri *(kid) and then served alongside. This slow cooking produces a surprisingly mild purée, as well as perfuming the meat. Garlic is often chopped very finely with parsley to produce a* persillade, *strewn raw over stuffed vegetables or stews, just before serving.*
ABOVE If you truly can't stand garlic (or its smell), lavender, the other pungent perfume of Provence can easily rise above it.

RIGHT The Bouches-du-Rhône encompasses variety in its history and landscape as well as in its food. The narrow streets of Cassis rise from a pretty, even though now touristy, small port tucked into one of the calanques (rocky inlets) east of Marseille.

RIGHT CENTRE Famous for its white wine, it is also home to a few of the dwindling number of fishermen who still use traditional nets to harvest the tiny rockfish used for soupe de poissons.

FAR RIGHT North-west of Cassis is Les Baux, the haunted medieval stronghold of the troubadours. Les Baux was destroyed during the fourteenth century and its ruins rise gaping and grey from the rock face.

RIGHT The Camargue is a vast flat stretch of lagoons and marshland, home to pink flamingoes, half-wild white horses and stocky black bulls. Mostly a nature reserve, the Camargue also produces rice and salt.

ABOVE The Bouches-du-Rhône is France's largest grower of the humble cabbage.

BOUCHES-DU-RHONE

Spread out across the broadening Rhône delta as the river sprawls its way to the sea, dividing into scores of streams to end in many mouths, Bouches-du-Rhône is aptly named. These have always been fertile plains, although it is only since the last century, with the arrival of irrigation and the railways, that the farmers were able to 'export' their produce north and that the region became prosperous as the market garden of France.

Roughly triangular, with its apex just south of Avignon and the Mediterranean as its base, the boundaries run south-west down the Rhône, and south-east down the Durance, then south to hit the sea east of the urban sprawl and ancient port of Marseille.

Here are some of the oldest towns in Provence. Marseille, founded by the Greeks over two and a half thousand years ago, is today bustling and industrial as France's principal port and second largest city. Aix-en-Provence, Marseille's near neighbour but opposite number, with its quiet elegance, ancient university and shaded seventeeth-century streets, was the Romans' first settlement when they invaded Gaul and once the capital of Provence. Arles, with its Roman amphitheatre still used for bull fights, but as famous for its association with van Gogh, is the central market for the agricultural riches of the *département*.

Here also, is some of Provence's most spectacular scenery: the mysterious marshes of the Camargue populated by semi-wild white horses, stocky black bulls and exotic pink flamingoes; the gentle hills of the Alpilles topped with jagged limestone teeth; the violent coastline of sheer cliffs corrugated with deep inlets called *calanques*; and Montagne Sainte-Victoire, painted so many times in so many lights by Aix-born Cézanne.

Here, indeed, is the famous Provençal light whose special luminosity Cézanne explored in his work, and which attracted some of France's most famous artists in the late nineteenth century. Ironically, it was a Dutchman, Vincent van Gogh who first saw the light. In 1888, he wrote that the future of modern art lay in the South of France. Van Gogh died soon afterwards but his name leads the long list of those that followed: Cézanne was a local boy, but Matisse, Picasso, Léger, Braque, Dufy, Seurat and Cocteau all settled in Provence, immortalizing it in their work. Since those days, artists' colonies have sprung up all over Provence: most, such as Gordes, are self-conscious enclaves where even the superlative quality of light will not disguise poor quality painting.

The region's agricultural bounty can be seen everywhere: orchards of almonds, cherries, pears, peaches, plums and figs; fields of artichokes, onions and just about any leafy

vegetable you can think of (most of France's cabbages are grown here). Vast polythene tunnels and glasshouses protect tomatoes, peppers and tender salad greens. The largest wholesale fruit and vegetable market in Europe is at Châteaurenard, south of Avignon in the Durance valley – itself one long market garden cut into patchwork by a series of irrigation canals. By nine o'clock every morning, literally tons of fresh produce is on its way to shops and restaurants all over the continent.

Olive groves flourish along the slopes and valleys of the Alpilles and eastwards to Salon-de-Provence, the traditional centre of the olive industry but now superseded by the small village of Mausanne-les-Alpilles. Here the olives, mostly Salonenque and Picholine, are picked green in the autumn and make a grassy, peppery, bright green oil which is now the favourite of Provence's chefs. This oil is cold-pressed in the traditional way at the seventeenth-century Moulin Jean-Marie Cornille and regularly wins awards at Paris fairs. Run as a co-operative, the Moulin has also started to promote a sort of 'olive oil *nouveau*' season with posters proclaiming 'the new olive oil has arrived'.

The great rival for these awards is one man: the very individual Henri Bellon in nearby Fontvieille. M. Bellon, who was the town's mayor for fifteen years until he pushed through a one-way system that the town needed but its shopkeepers didn't want, is very proud of his new, automatic machinery. One of the grand old men of olive oil production, he proudly stuck a Paris 1992 Gold Medal label on the bottle of the deep-green oil he presented to me. Begun by his grandfather in 1870, his enterprise makes a modest fifty thousand litres of oil from twelve hectares of olives picked black in November and December. The secret of his olive oil, he said, lies not in the machinery at his mill, Les Bédarrides, but in his head and in the quality and combination of different olive varieties. And, he added, all must be tranquil and gentle both in the crushing of the olives and in his mind.

THE GRASS IS GREENER?

Along the slopes of the Alpilles hills and on the Crau Plain which they bisect, sheep can be seen grazing. A breed of merino, they rival their more famous alpine relative, the Sisteron, from Alpes-de-Haute-Provence, for taste. Their succulence comes from their pasture; it gives the meat such a special flavour that it has been seriously suggested the grass be protected by an *appellation contrôlée*. In the summer the flocks move to higher pastures – not, these days, by the traditional migratory trek but simply bundled into lorries. They return the same way for winter and lambing. Not many male lambs make it past Easter except as *gigots* at the paschal feast, but sheep's testicles are sometimes spotted in the market at Tarascon (although its magnificent castle rising straight out of the Rhône is probably a more popular reason to make the visit).

Goats' milk is turned into cheese, though the most famous *chèvre* of its kind, and another example of not letting anything go to waste, is now rare. This is Brousse du Rove, a round, ricotta-like cheese traditionally made from the whey of the *rove*, a brown, large-horned goat. As the whey, left over from the normal full-fat *chèvre*, was heated, the solids coming to the

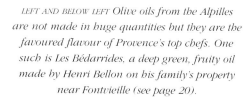

LEFT AND BELOW LEFT Olive oils from the Alpilles are not made in huge quantities but they are the favoured flavour of Provence's top chefs. One such is Les Bédarrides, a deep green, fruity oil made by Henri Bellon on his family's property near Fontvieille (see page 20).

surface were skimmed off and drained through muslin into a three-legged earthenware vessel, lightly beaten (*brousse*) and drained again in moulds to produce 175-grams balls. The seasonal arrival of Brousse du Rove used to be such an important event that it was cried around the streets of Marseille but, sadly, the breed has been replaced with more prolific, and more cost-effective, milk producers. Patrick Rance, the great cheese guru who lives nearby for part of each year, knows of only two small herds of *roves* that are still in existence: one at Sambuc and another at Raphèle-les-Arcs. Brousse du Rove made of sheep's or cows' milk is more common today, although it is still often eaten in the traditional way, sprinkled with sugar and orange flower water. It has the reputation of making children sleep and be well-behaved; adults still eat it for lunch with oil, vinegar, garlic, herbs and onion.

ABOVE The spirit of romance is deeply imbued in the Alpilles around Les Baux. The Val d'Enfer (Hell Valley) is a jagged gorge, pock-marked by caves which used to be inhabited. Though no longer lived in by human beings, they are reputed to be the homes of witches and fairies.
ABOVE LEFT Nearby in Fontvieille is Daudet's Mill, named after the nineteenth-century Provençal author of tales of local life. The most famous, Letters from my Mill, was inspired by this former flour mill, now a museum.

ABOVE LEFT AND LEFT *Great lunar landscapes of salt edge the Camargue delta, while an increasing area of marshland has been reclaimed for growing long-grain rice.*
ABOVE *Further inland, black bulls bred for fighting rather than meat, graze.*
BELOW *Semi-wild white horses are an ancient feature of the Camargue.*
FAR LEFT *The cowboys live in traditional* cabanes, *decorated with skulls of former fighting bulls.*

Unlike elsewhere in Provence, there is local beef. But it is from the tough Camarguaise bulls once their fighting days are over. Some of the *gardians*, the cowboys of the region who are as tough as the cattle they herd, grill the meat over wood fires. But most is slow-cooked as daubes or used in sausages. The unique *saucisson d'Arles* should be made with three-quarters lean pork and one-quarter beef (tradition has it that some donkey meat should be mixed in, as well). Beef also means that one of the few cheeses traditionally made with cows' milk can be found here. Tomme de Camargue is a small round or log-shaped cheese, often coated in thyme or *sarriette* but rarely found outside the region.

The *gardians* share the Camargue with the gypsies who gather in May at Saintes-Maries-de-la-Mer, their spiritual home. Legend has it that Mary Magdalene and the Virgin Mary's stepsisters (both also called Mary and the mothers of disciples) fled into exile here in a small boat, landed on the beach, and spent their last years in Provence. With them came Sarah, a black servant girl. Mary Magdalene moved on to Les Baux, but the other two Marys and Sarah settled where they landed. Sarah became the gypsies' patron saint, while the tomb of the two Marys became a popular pilgrimage. Gypsies from all over the world still congregate here every year on 25th and 26th May for a great fête. The richly-dressed statue of Sarah, escorted by the *gardians* on horseback, is paraded through the streets surrounded by gypsies in traditional costume. The rest of the time is filled with dancing, horse-racing and bull-running. On 3rd June they all get down to business at their annual horse fair.

The Camargue also has a tradition of rice culture, although the old short-grained rice, mostly used for cattle feed, has given way to long-grained rice, much of it organically grown for the table. The original industry, introduced by Spaniards in the fourteenth century, had almost died out by the start of the Second World War but, in 1947, encouraged by the government and with the help of experts from Indochina, great irrigation and drainage programmes were begun, paddy fields were rebuilt and new strains of rice introduced. Arles, the rice capital, now hosts an annual rice fair every September.

The irrigation and drainage schemes have also produced more arable land, but much of the Camargue is a nature reserve, a still-empty, marshy plain, studded with lagoons and the small, but distinctive thatch-roofed *cabanes* of the *gardians*, their low, whitewashed walls curved at one end. But its shoreline is given over to an ancient industry. Here, vast natural salt beds, or *salins*, have been producing their vital mineral since Roman times. Today, over a million metric tonnes are extracted annually from ten thousand hectares, all owned by the Salins du Midi. The salt is 'harvested' between August and October and piled into *camelles* (mountains, sometimes twenty metres high, of white crystals glinting in the sun). When seen from a distance, the effect is of an almost lunar landscape.

At one edge of this off-white desert, in sandy fingers around the Golfe du Lion, vines make a surprise appearance. They have been there for over a century, making Listel, or *vins des sables* (the vines are rooted in the sand), a light, refreshing rosé. The vineyards are centred on the medieval walled town of Aigues-Mortes. Fortified by King Louis IX (Saint Louis) in 1248, Aigues-Mortes is today landlocked three miles from the sea. The salt in Aigues-Mortes came in useful two centuries after King Louis when the bodies of Burgundian invaders were thrown into an empty tower and salted to preserve them until their victors could bury them.

PASTIS

Pastis *is the quintessential Provençal aperitif. The drink is based on anise, a plant with a long history of restorative and digestive powers. At some unknown time, so the story goes, a man lived in a hut in the Lubéron forest. A great plague, which caused an unquenchable thirst, struck the region. Its only cure proved to be a potion the man brewed from herbs. Once the plague had subsided, the man left for Marseille and sold his drink in a bar called* 'Au Bonhomme Passe-soif' ('The Good-Natured Thirst Quencher'). Passe-soif *became* passe-sitis, *and then* pastis. *What is known, is that its nineteenth-century equivalent,* absinthe, *also contained wormwood. In 1915, when the government decided that it made drinkers incapable of fighting in, or making arms for, the First World War,* absinthe *and all anise-based drinks were banned. When, in 1932, wormwood-free anise drinks were once again permitted, one of the first into the field was Paul Ricard. Ricard is richer, deeper and more subtle than its main rival Pernod (now also owned by Ricard).*

SERGE PIRO, FISHERMAN

*Every morning, two or three small
boats leave the harbour at Carry-le-Rouet, just
west of Marseille. These are all that
remain of a fishing fleet that supported
twenty-seven families thirty years ago. It comes
as something of a surprise to find one
of them captained by a young man, but Serge
Piro (above right) took over the boat Notre-
Dame-du-Rouet from his father five years ago
determined, in his words, to 'conserve'
fishing as a viable way of life. He and his friends
want to make Carry and its surrounding
bays into a little refuge. 'Already we
are careful not to overfish because we want
there to be enough for future generations',
he declares. Most fishermen along this coast
sell direct to the giant co-operative
in Marseille, but M. Piro prefers to sell his
catch, on average ten kilos of red mullet and
other rockfish, directly from his boat to
local restaurateurs.*

FISH FOR COMPLIMENTS

Needless to say, the salt beds' preservative qualities have been put to more conventional uses, one resulting in two of Provence's most famous dishes. Cod is not a Mediterranean fish but it has been a part of Provence's diet for centuries. It was probably brought dried, as stockfish, by Vikings to be exchanged for oil. A few hundred years later, when Europe discovered the vast fishing grounds off Newfoundland, the cod was preserved in salt for the long journey home. Fishermen sailed to Aigues-Mortes for salt, bartering already-salted fish in return. The Provençaux soaked the fish and poached it. Served whole, surrounded by a vibrant mixture of young vegetables and accompanied by large bowls of *aïoli*, it became the centrepiece of the *grand aïoli*, the famous festive platter of Provence (see page 62). Puréed with their other great natural resource, olive oil, it produces *brandade de morue*.

The Mediterranean has always provided a rich harvest of fresh fish. For eating whole, *loup de mer*, or sea bass, is the undisputed king, but fish stalls glisten with *dorade*, sea bream, John Dory, snapper, *rascasse* (essential to the mighty *bouillabaisse*, see pages 27, 118), red and grey mullet and tuna as well as heaps of the myriad-coloured tiny rockfish to be stewed and then puréed into *soupe de poissons* (see page 80). There will be octopus, squid and, sometimes, tiny cuttlefish. Local mussels and spider crabs are familiar crustacea but, in season, there are also sea urchins, tiny crabs called *favouilles,* and *tellines* (pebble-like clams). Sardines and anchovies, fresh in season, salted for the rest of the year, are ancient staples. But whatever they are and however they are cooked, there is one inviolable Provençal rule: fish might live in water but they should die in olive oil.

In spite of the appearance of bounty, however, the Mediterranean is badly overfished. Even in Marseille, the fish stalls along the Quai des Belges can sometimes only muster a sparse selection: in the smaller ports along the coast, perhaps only two or three local boats can make a living. And the fish are smaller. M. Jean Garde, a retired chef living in Martigues, says that the fish he used for *bouillabaisse* twenty years ago were so large that they had to be cut in chunks. Today, he can use many of the same species whole.

He, and others, tell a similar story about *oursins*, or sea urchins. During their short season from January to the end of March, they were so cheap and plentiful people could – and did – gorge on their rich pink roe, making a meal of them washed down with, 'always a little too much' rosé wine. Today, he mourns, they are fewer, smaller, contain less roe and have been priced into luxury. 'Parisians now scoop out the roe daintily with coffee spoons,' he said. 'We used to just wipe round the insides with bread.'

Martigues, north of Marseille on a spit of land between the sea and the large freshwater lake, the Etang de Berre, was once a small fishing port famous for *poutarge*, the pressed roe of the grey mullet, also known as Caviar de Martigues (see page 25). Sadly it, too, has become a rare and expensive delicacy. Martigues, the town, is composed of three former villages: Jonquières, Ile Saint-Genest and Ferrières, a merger that has given it a firm place in French history. When the villages joined forces over four hundred years ago, they also combined their colours to form a red (Jonquières), white (Ile Saint-Genest) and blue (Ferrières) flag. It was this, they say, which became the Revolutionary *tricolore*.

ABOVE The old town of Martigues retains some of the special charm which attracted painters and writers in the nineteenth century and made it into something of a literary and artistic landmark.
RIGHT Tellines are tiny, pebble-shaped clams specific to the Camargue.
BELOW RIGHT Anchovies used to be scooped up in great shoals all along the coast but, although still plentiful, they are fewer than they were.
BELOW Sudden squalls along the Mediterranean can often bring fishing to a halt.

POUTARGUE

The poutargue fisherman pictured above awaits good fishing weather in his hut on the port of Martigues. Poutargue is the salted, pressed and dried roe of the grey mullet, or muge. It is an ancient snack which used to be found all round the Mediterranean. In France, it became a famous delicacy called Caviar de Martigues after the small fishing port just west of Marseille. Today, grey mullet is increasingly rare, knocked out by the pollution from the huge industrial zone which surrounds the Etang de Berre behind Martigues.
In July, when the fish are ready to spawn, they swim from the sea to the lake through the Canal de Coronte which bisects Martigues. Fishermen traditionally laid nets across the canal, separated the female mullet from the catch and removed the roe. Then the women salted the roes and weighted them to press out moisture. Most of the poutargue sold these days is coated in wax, a sign that it is imported from north Africa.

RIGHT Picasso spent his last years at Château Vauvenargues near Aix-en-Provence.
BELOW Les Deux Garçons is probably one of the most famous cafés on the Cours Mirabeau.
FAR RIGHT, ABOVE Calissons are iced, almond-paste lozenges and a speciality of Aix-en-Provence.
OPPOSITE LEFT The placid, old port of Marseille belies the hustle of France's oldest city.
FAR RIGHT, BELOW Marseille is home to such cosmopolitan enclaves as this Arab spice market.

BOUILLABAISSE

The great fish stew of Marseille, bouillabaisse *courts controversy. Originally a mixture of water and olive oil boiled up by fishermen in cauldrons over wood fires to cook the fish they could not sell,* bouillabaisse *today is an expensive dish in restaurants all along the coast of Provence. Although water and olive oil are always the essential basics, most restaurants now add rockfish to make an intense broth very like* soupe de poissons, *before briefly cooking whole white fish to make a two-part dish.*

Just what fish should be used is an open question, although there is general agreement that there should be at least four. Mussels can be allowed but lobster and other luxury crustacea, never! Some Marseille restaurateurs abide by a self-imposed Bouillabaisse Charter *which states that the choice should be scorpion fish (*rascasse*), weever fish, monkfish, John Dory and conger eel.* Rascasse *is thought essential because it is supposed to bring out the flavours of the other fish. The two really important points are that the broth must boil (*bouillir*) briskly to emulsify the oil and water, then, with the heat lowered (*abaissée*), the whole fish are added. Saffron is essential, and some chefs add tomatoes. 'Who told you no tomatoes?' sniffed one. 'Must have been a Parisian.'*

Both Marseille and Martigues are now surrounded by the huge industrial zone that rings the Etang de Berre and seems to spread ever outwards towards Aix-en-Provence, only thirty kilometres to the north. But Aix retains the gentility that always set it apart from its cruder, more boisterous, neighbour on the coast. With its important history as an ancient spa and cultural centre, Aix has an intellectual air, a period charm, a self-containedness which, for many people, captures the essence of Provence. I can't help but admire the shady elegance of the Cours Mirabeau, that broad boulevard punctuated with gentle fountains and lined with elegant townhouses, but I think Aix sounds a great deal more fun five hundred years ago when René d'Anjou, one-time King of Naples and Duke of Provence, ruled at court. He encouraged artists and playwrights, revived festivals and, not least in the eyes of the Provençaux who still revere him, introduced the muscat grape to Provence. Indeed, it is this one of his many achievements that is remembered in his statue on the Cours Mirabeau where he stands for all time, a bunch of muscat grapes in one hand.

In Bouches-du-Rhône, as elsewhere in Provence, there is little tradition of desserts as such. But the sweet-toothed are not ignored. As well as crystallized fruits, made around the town of Saint-Rémy-de-Provence (Aix-en-Provence produces *calissons*. These are lozenge-shaped sweets made from ground almond paste). Aix was once the site of Provence's main almond market, and is now Europe's largest centre for the processed nut. The almond paste is mixed with chopped crystallized melon and topped with royal icing. Anyone familiar with the traditional English Christmas cake topping of iced marzipan will know the taste; the melon flavour is often hard to discern. Made for over three hundred and fifty years, the sweets now have their own guild and their own *appellation*.

ABOVE *Arles, built by the Romans on the banks of the Rhône, is the architectural, economic and agricultural centre of Bouches-du-Rhône.*
RIGHT *Arles boasts the grandeur of a Roman theatre and an arcaded first century amphitheatre still used for bullfights. It is also home to an annual arts festival. Its Saturday market, stretching for several kilometres along the city's main boulevard, is the largest and best in all Provence.*
LEFT, FROM BOTTOM *Country breads, herbs and spices and the local speciality, saucissons d'Arles, are all to be found at Arles market. The sausages are spicy and contain mainly pork, and sometimes beef from Camarguaise bulls.*

TO MARKET, TO MARKET

The best market, and the most famous in Provence, is at Arles every Saturday. Then, the long boulevard de Lices (don't scratch, it means the lists used in jousting) is crowded with stalls, all organized into sections: plants, bric-à-brac, clothing and, of course, food. Here are the freshest of fruits and vegetables and, it might be said, even fresher meat. Fowls cackle angrily in baskets and rabbits look soulfully through their wire cages. Here are olives in all their manifestations, an almost infinite variety of honeys, herbs, spices, and a host of dried leaves and flowers for soothing or restorative *tisanes*. There are the fresh goats' cheeses straight from the farm, mobile butchers' shops with their own versions of *veritables saucissons d'Arles* and the fish stalls with one woman selling only tiny clams known as *tellines*. It was here I found my first *poutargue*, so expensive I was sure I'd got the real thing. But it was coated with wax as an additional preservative so, as retired chef, M. Garde, pointed out when I proudly showed it to him, it was definitely not from Martigues.

The Wednesday market at Saint-Rémy-de-Provence is a compact version of Arles in a more beautiful setting. The birthplace of Nostrodamus, the sixteenth-century doctor, astronomer and prophet, Saint-Rémy is a picture-postcard town, the synthesis of Provence with narrow cobbled streets leading to tinkling fountains in every square, as well as broad, tree-shaded boulevards. In spite of heavy tourist traffic you can still see how Vincent van Gogh found a measure of peace in his last year spent (as a voluntary patient) at the nearby Priory of Saint-Paul-de-Mausole. Saint-Rémy is a town of gardeners in the midst of a sea of market gardens and specializes in the production of seeds. Perhaps because of this, the market has a more artisan quality than any other I know. Even the cheap clothing seems to have been aesthetically selected and there are stalls selling plain olive-wood bowls and utensils (the general tendency is to intricate, over-wrought carving) and brightly glazed conical earthenware *tians* traditionally used for steeping fruit to be crystallized.

LEFT Rowing boats moored alongside the quay at Cassis look like frail craft for local fishermen. But most boats fish no more than three hundred metres from the coastline in search of the tiny rockfish essential to a true soupe de poissons. *They may look small but, I was told, they are better than larger boats for the Mediterranean which 'has smaller waves than other seas'! Besides, the fishermen admit, they don't put out in bad weather. Small fishermen such as these are a dying breed and Cassis now relies on tourism and the income from its wine, especially its dry, flinty white, thought by many to be the best in Provence.*
ABOVE LEFT One of the best known wines from Cassis is Clos Sainte-Magdeleine, one of a scattering of small vineyards terraced within the folds of the steep hills rising from the port. Since the whole appellation *can make only half a million bottles a year, it is rarely seen far away from its home region.*
ABOVE RIGHT Seen all over the world today, however, is Perrier, the naturally sparkling mineral water bottled in seemingly inexhaustible quantities at its source at Vergèze, near Nîmes.

TOP Geographically, Nîmes is part of Languedoc, but culturally its place is in Provence. Its Roman origins are proclaimed by its amphitheatre, a twin of that at Arles and still used for bullfights. But for all its past prestige, Nîmes is a modern city. It recovered remarkably well from flash-floods in 1988 which left the city devastated. ABOVE Aside from being a centre of the olive industry, Nîmes has more modern gastronomic quirks. The recently invented Clous de Nîmes are chocolate truffles stamped with the city's symbol of a chained crocodile.

The strong Arab influence in the Bouches-du-Rhône, dating from its ancient trading with north Africa, was greatly reinforced in the early 1960s after Algerian independence. So, it is not uncommon to find cinnamon, cumin, chick peas, pistachios or raisins spiking dishes, and couscous is a great favourite among all age groups. Indeed, in his *La Cuisinière Provençale*, published in 1895, the chef Jean-Baptiste Reboul published a recipe for couscous on the grounds of its popularity. Few markets are without their stalls selling all these products: Marseille has its own Arab market around the Place des Capucins.

Nîmes is also known for its plump, green, stuffed olives, claims *brandade de morue* as its own and has given its name to what must be the world's most-worn textile – denim (fabric *de Nîmes*). The town was founded by the Romans around a sacred spring, but the water we know Nîmes for – and which the Romans seem to have missed – is just a few kilometres south-west in Vergèze, the source of *eau*-so-sparkling and now *eau*-so-famous Perrier. This naturally sparkling mineral water was once owned by a member of the Harmsworth newspaper dynasty. Partly paralyzed, his physiotherapy involved swinging Indian clubs of the kind used by jugglers – from which came the shape of the now-familiar green bottle. The water comes from an underground lake but the 'source' is a rather disappointing burble of water clad in a plastic dome like a roadside shrine.

WINES OF BOUCHES-DU-RHONE

The wines of Provence have never had cachet, mostly because the strong sun has produced large quantites of high-alcohol wine. Whites were inevitably flabby, reds tough and headache-inducing – hence the predominance of rosés of varying quality. But good wines do exist in the Bouches-du-Rhône.

Cassis (not to be confused with the blackcurrant liqueur from Dijon) is among the best. Vines have been grown above Cassis, the pretty port just east of Marseille, since Greek times. The vineyards are planted in sloping pockets between rocky cliffs that fall into a necklace of deep inlets. Until a century ago, most of the wine produced was a red muscat, today it is best known for a flinty, dry white wine, exceptional for Provence. The two best-known wines are Domaine du Paternel and Clos Sainte-Magdeleine although with an *appellation* that dictates a maximum of five hundred thousand bottles (including some rosé) from the one hundred and twenty hectares of vines per year, Cassis is rarely seen abroad.

Côteaux d'Aix-en-Provence spreads eastward into the Var. This was the first area of France to grow vines and over four hundred thousand hectares produce reds, whites and rosés. The reds are particularly good, ranging from light, fruity wines to drink young, to more tannic wines that repay bottle age. To the west, around the haunted ruins of Les Baux, a sub-division, Coteaux des Baux-en-Provence, makes increasingly good reds based on Cabernet and Syrah grapes. Close to Aix itself is the miniscule *appellation* of Palette, hidden in woods off the autoroute. Almost the only producer is Château Simone which makes a complex red wine that is spicy – and pricey. Made from the same grape varieties as Côtes du Rhône, it is aged in beer barrels for three years, then bottled.

L'ESCALE

PROMENADE DU PORT, 13620 CARRY-LE-ROUET, TEL 42 45 00 47

L'Escale and the family Clor must have one of the all-time great views. Perched halfway up a cliff above the tiny picture-postcard fishing village of Carry-le-Rouet, they look over boats bobbing in the small natural harbour and out to the Mediterranean beyond. Carry remains amazingly unspoiled and a few fishermen still land their catch every morning. For chef-patron Gérard Clor, it's just a few minutes walk down the cliffside every morning to the freshest possible fish for his restaurant. Diners sit out on a terrace or behind plate-glass windows in a setting that is palpably romantic – it's impossible to accept that you are only fifteen minutes away from the autoroute from Marseille.

We sat on the terrace after a long Sunday lunch, wondering if we should book a room. 'Sorry', M. Clor said, 'we are only a restaurant'. 'But, what about ...?' I asked, waving my arms at the imposing pink-stucco building just yards across a patio. 'That', came the reply, 'is my home'. I have never felt envy like it.

TARTE AUX FRAISES ET AUX AMANDES

Strawberry and Almond Tart

The ground almonds in this tart help bring out the flavour of the fresh strawberries. (Illustrated right)

SERVES 6

100g/3 ½ oz butter, softened
100g/3 ½ oz ground almonds
100g/3 ½ oz icing sugar, sifted
2 eggs, lightly beaten
Kirsch
225g/8oz strawberries, hulled and
halved lengthways

FOR THE PATE SUCREE

100g/3 ½ oz butter, softened
55g/2oz caster sugar
2 egg yolks, lightly beaten
200g/7oz plain flour
1tbsp chilled water

FOR THE CREME PATISSIERE

2 egg yolks
45g/1 ½ oz caster sugar
15g/ ½ oz flour
175ml/6fl oz milk
½ vanilla pod, split

To make the *pâte sucrée*, put the butter and sugar in a bowl and beat together until pale yellow. Beat in the egg yolks and mix together well. Gradually add the flour and mix thoroughly to make a dough. Add the water and knead until smooth, then form into a ball, wrap in cling film and chill for 1-2 hours.

Meanwhile, to make the *crème pâtissière*, put the egg yolks and about one-third of the sugar in a bowl and whisk until the mixture turns pale yellow and forms a ribbon when the whisk is lifted. Sift in the flour and stir together well. Put the milk, the rest of the sugar and the vanilla pod into a saucepan and bring to the boil. Immediately pour half of the milk on to the egg and sugar mixture, stirring constantly. Stir in the rest of the milk and return to the pan, remove the vanilla pod and gently bring to the boil, stirring constantly. Still stirring, cook at the gentlest boil for about 2 minutes. Spoon the mixture into a bowl and set aside to cool.

Roll out the dough to make a 22cm/8 ½ in circle, 6mm/ ¼ in thick and place in a loose-based tart tin. Crimp up the edges to make a rim, about 2cm/ ¾ in high. Trim the edges and chill for 20 minutes.

Combine the butter, almonds and icing sugar together in a bowl, then mix in the eggs.

Preheat the oven to 180°C/350°F/gas mark 4.

Remove the *pâte sucrée* base from the fridge. Beat the *crème pâtissière* well, then stir 3 tablespoons into the ground almond mixture, beat well again, and pour into the base not quite to the top. Bake for 30 minutes, until lightly browned. Remove from the oven and allow to rest for 10 minutes, then slide on to a wire rack to cool.

Spread the rest of the *crème pâtissière* over the filling and arrange the strawberries on top. Sprinkle with Kirsch and serve.

LE VACCARES

PLACE DU FORUM, 13200 ARLES, TEL 90 96 06 17

Bernard Dumas thinks Provençal, speaks Provençal and cooks Provençal. The keeper of the culinary flame of traditional dishes followed in his father's footsteps in 1961 and now his own son is almost ready to follow suit. M. Dumas' restaurant, Le Vaccarès, on the Place du Forum right in the ancient heart of Arles, is named after the giant lagoon and nature reserve in the nearby Camargue. The choice of name is an apt one, for M. Dumas's way of cooking keeps tradition alive, rather than merely preserving it. Unlike many chefs who 'modernize' traditional dishes beyond recognition, M. Dumas, a serious man but with a distinct twinkle in his eye, uses original recipes, presented simply but with flair. The restaurant's other claim to fame is its first-floor terrace, which features in one of Vincent van Gogh's most famous paintings, Le Café de la Nuit, perhaps better known as the 'starry, starry night' painting.

BEIGNETS DE BRANDADE DE MORUE

Salt Cod Fritters
(Illustrated left)

SERVES 4
450g/1lb salt cod
300ml/10fl oz extra virgin olive oil
100ml/3 ½ fl oz milk
2 garlic cloves, very finely chopped
2-3tbsp double cream
freshly ground black pepper
freshly grated nutmeg
vegetable oil, for deep-frying
***rouille*, to serve (see page 34)**
lemon wedges, to serve

FOR THE BATTER
300g/10 ½ oz plain flour
pinch of salt
8g/ ¼ oz fresh yeast
500ml/16fl oz lager or
light beer
2tbsp olive oil
1 egg, lightly beaten
3 extra egg whites

A day and a half ahead, put the salt cod in a large bowl, cover with cold water and soak for 36 hours, changing the water every 6 hours.

At least 2 or 3 hours before you want to deep-fry the beignets, prepare the batter. Put the flour and salt into a mixing bowl, make a well in the centre and crumble the yeast into the well. Pour the lager or beer into a saucepan and warm it to blood temperature, but no higher. Pour the lager into the dry ingredients, add the oil and the beaten egg and gradually incorporate the flour into the liquid to make a smooth, thin batter. Leave to rest in a warm place for 2-3 hours. Prepare the *rouille* and chill until needed.

Remove the salt cod from the soaking liquid and put into a deep saucepan. Add enough fresh water to cover and slowly bring to a medium boil and cook for 15 minutes.

Meanwhile, heat the olive oil and milk in separate pans without letting the milk boil.

Drain the salt cod and when cool, remove the skin and flake the flesh into a large bowl. Add the garlic and beat with a wooden spoon. Continue beating and steadily add the olive oil and milk. Beat in enough cream to make the mixture smooth. Add the seasoning.

When ready to deep-fry, whisk the egg whites until stiff, then fold them into the batter.

Heat enough oil for deep-frying in a heavy-based saucepan over a high heat until a small cube of dry bread browns in 20 seconds. Use a soup spoon to roll the salt cod mixture into 16-20 balls and set them aside. Fry a few balls at a time until they are golden brown. Drain well. Serve with *rouille* and lemon wedges.

SOUPE DE CERISES AU VIN ROUGE ET A LA GLACE DE REGLISSE

Cherry and Red Wine Soup with Liquorice Ice-Cream

Bernard Dumas's soup can be served either on its own as a starter or as a dessert with the liquorice ice-cream. You can substitute a confectioner's liquorice stick for the liquorice powder, if you wish. (Illustrated right)

SERVES 4

FOR THE LIQUORICE ICE-CREAM

(makes about 500g/1lb)

4 egg yolks

85g/3oz sugar

350ml/12fl oz milk

½ vanilla pod, split

1tbsp liquorice powder

***or* 1x55g/2oz liquorice stick, finely chopped**

FOR THE CHERRY AND RED WINE SOUP

1 litre/1 ¾ pt fruity red wine, such as Lirac

200g/7oz sugar

1 cinnamon stick

1 sprig rosemary

25g/ ¾ oz butter

1kg/2 ¾ lb black cherries, stoned

fresh mint leaves, to garnish

First of all, prepare the ice-cream. Put the egg yolks and 30g/1oz of the sugar in a bowl and whisk until pale yellow.

Put the milk, vanilla pod, the chopped liquorice stick, if using, and the remaining sugar in a saucepan and bring to the boil, stirring until the liquorice dissolves. Pour over the egg mixture, whisking constantly.

Return the mixture to the pan and heat gently, stirring with a wooden spoon until the custard is thick enough to coat the back of it. Do not boil or the eggs will curdle. Strain into a bowl and set aside to cool, stirring occasionally. Then stir in the liquorice powder, if using, pour into an ice-cream maker and churn until frozen. Chill until ready to serve.

Put the wine, sugar, cinnamon and rosemary in a saucepan and bring to the boil.

Melt the butter in a deep sauté pan over a medium heat, then add the cherries and cook, stirring occasionally, until lightly browned. Strain in the hot spiced wine through a sieve, then simmer over a medium heat for about 15 minutes. Use a slotted spoon to transfer the cherries to a serving dish and keep warm.

Increase the heat under the sauté pan and return the wine to the boil, then continue boiling until it reduces almost to a syrup.

Arrange the cherries in 4 deep soup plates, then pour the hot wine over. Add a scoop of liquorice ice-cream to each serving and decorate with mint leaves. Serve immediately.

AIOLI

Garlic Mayonnaise

This is Provence. It makes a wonderful accompaniment to fish soups and, of course, is an essential part of Grand Aïoli, *the great feast dish of every family and village fête (see page 62). I've used the traditional quantity of two cloves of garlic per person, but you can use more or less depending on your own taste – though there's not much point in making this unless it packs a powerful punch. But do bear in mind that Provençal garlic has a milder taste than that grown further north and that fresh garlic is gentler than dried.*

SERVES 4
8 cloves garlic, peeled
1 slice fresh white bread,
crust removed
1tsp Dijon mustard
200ml/7fl oz extra virgin olive oil
1tbsp white wine vinegar
2 egg yolks
200ml/7fl oz sunflower or groundnut oil
salt and freshly ground black pepper

Put the garlic in a food processor and process until finely chopped. Add the bread to the chopped garlic and process quickly until crumbs begin to form, then add the mustard and salt and pepper.

With the motor running, add 1 tablespoon of the olive oil, the vinegar and egg yolks through the feed tube. With the motor still running, add the remaining olive oil and the sunflower oil in a slow, steady stream until a thick mayonnaise forms. Season with salt and pepper according to taste. Transfer the *aïoli* to a bowl and serve immediately or cover with film and chill until required.

ROUILLE

Pepper and Garlic Sauce with Saffron

Another basic of Provençal cuisine, rouille has similarities to aïoli but should not be confused with it. The red colouring can come from pimientos, or more simply, as here, from cayenne pepper. Saffron is essential. Rouille is traditionally served with bouillabaisse *(see pages 27, 118) and made at the same time, using a little stock or broth from the soup.*

SERVES 4
4 garlic cloves, peeled
1 slice fresh white bread,
crust removed
1 small potato, boiled, peeled and mashed
1tsp cayenne pepper
½ tsp saffron threads
100ml/3½ oz extra virgin olive oil
3tbsp fish stock
1 egg yolk
100ml/3½ fl oz sunflower or groundnut oil

Put the garlic in a food processor and process until finely chopped. Add the bread to the chopped garlic and process quickly until crumbs begin to form, then add the mashed potato, cayenne pepper and saffron and process again quickly until all the ingredients are well blended together.

With the motor running, add 1 tablespoon of the olive oil, 1 tablespoon of the fish stock and the egg yolk through the feed tube. With the motor still running, add the remaining olive oil and the sunflower oil in a slow, steady stream until a thick mayonnaise forms, then add the remaining fish stock. Transfer to a bowl and serve immediately or cover with film and chill until required.

FENOUILS A LA BOHEMIENNE

Fennel Cooked Bohemian Style

Fennel is one of the most distinctive flavourings in Provençal food and it is an essential part of a bouquet garni. This dish is based on la Bohémienne, *which is Marseille's version of* ratatouille. Bohémienne *means gypsy, though no one knows why the name has become associated with this style of dish.*

SERVES 4
4 fennel bulbs, trimmed and quartered
lengthways
2 courgettes, trimmed and quartered
lengthways
1 large onion, sliced into
thin rings
2 garlic cloves, halved
4tbsp extra virgin olive oil
2tbsp flat-leaf parsley, finely chopped
salt and freshly ground black pepper

Preheat the oven to 200°C/400°F/gas mark 6.

Bring a large saucepan of water to the boil over a high heat. Put the fennel, courgettes, onion and garlic in a steamer and place on top of the boiling water. Cover and steam for 6 minutes.

Meanwhile, cut out 4 squares of aluminium foil, each large enough to hold one-quarter of the vegetables. Divide the vegetables between the pieces of foil and sprinkle with olive oil and the finely-chopped parsley, then wrap up into parcels. Make sure all the edges are sealed. Place on a baking sheet, put in the oven and cook for 20 minutes.

Do not unwrap the parcels until they are brought to the table, so the full aroma can be appreciated when they are opened.

RATATOUILLE

Provençal Vegetable Stew
(Illustrated left)

SERVES 4
200ml/7fl oz olive oil
225g/8oz onions, thinly sliced
2 garlic cloves, crushed
225g/8oz tomatoes, peeled, seeded, chopped
bouquet garni consisting of bay leaf, thyme
and a stalk of fennel
250ml/8fl oz white wine,
such as Côtes de Provence
350g/12oz aubergines, cut into
2 ½ cm/1in dice
225g/8oz courgettes, cut into
2 ½ cm/1in dice
225g/8oz red peppers, peeled, cored and cut
into strips
5 fresh mint or basil leaves, shredded
salt and freshly ground black pepper

Heat about 3 ½ tablespoons of oil over a low heat. Add the onions and cook until soft, stirring occasionally. Add the garlic, tomatoes, bouquet garni and half the wine and simmer, uncovered, over a low heat, for 30-45 minutes.

Heat half the remaining oil in another large pan. Add the aubergines and courgettes and cook over a medium heat, adding more oil as necessary and stirring often, until the aubergines begin to soften. Drain well.

Add the aubergines, courgettes and peppers to the tomato mixture, then stir in the remaining wine and bring to the boil. Add the seasoning, cover the pan and cook, over a very low heat, for 45 minutes to 1 hour.

Remove the bouquet garni, adjust the seasoning if necessary, and transfer the *ratatouille* to a large bowl. Scatter with the shredded mint or basil leaves.

BOURRIDE

Fish Stew with Creamy Garlic Sauce

Regarded by many (including myself) as superior to bouillabaisse, bourride *is classic, elegant and rich. It can be made with any firm, white fish but, as always, freshness is all.*

SERVES 4
300g/10 ½ oz *aïoli* (see page 34)
1tbsp olive oil
4 garlic cloves, very finely chopped
½ carrot, thinly sliced
½ courgette, thinly sliced
¼ leek, thinly sliced in rings
4 firm white fish fillets of 150g/5 ½ oz each,
such as monkfish, turbot, sea bass,
sea bream, whiting or grey mullet
1 bay leaf
sprig of thyme
1l/1 ¾ pt fish stock
12-16 small new potatoes
2 egg yolks, lightly beaten
fresh herbs, to garnish
garlic croutons, to serve

Make the *aïoli* and chill until needed.

Heat the olive oil in a wide sauté pan or frying pan over a medium heat. Add the garlic, carrot, courgette and leek and quickly fry without letting them colour. Place the fish fillets on top, then add the herbs and pour in the stock. Cover the pan, lower the heat and poach for 15 minutes until the flesh flakes easily when tested with the tip of a knife.

Meanwhile, put the potatoes in a saucepan of lightly salted water and bring to the boil. Lower the heat and cook until tender. Drain and when cool enough to handle, peel the potatoes. Set aside and keep warm.

Use a fish slice to transfer the fish fillets to 4 warmed, deep soup plates, then cover each and keep warm.

Strain the cooking stock into a clean saucepan, then bring to the boil and continue boiling until reduced by half.

Put 200g/7oz of the *aïoli* in a bowl and stir in one egg yolk and a ladleful of the reduced cooking stock. Once everything is well blended, add the remaining egg yolk and another ladleful of stock. Pour this mixture into the remaining stock in the saucepan and cook over a medium heat until the mixture thickens. Do not boil.

Divide the broth evenly between the soup plates and garnish each with herbs. Serve the boiled potatoes, the remaining *aïoli* and the garlic croutons on the side for each person to add their own.

BAUDROIE A L'AIGO SAU

Monkfish Soup

Baudroie *is Provençal for* lotte, *which, in turn, is French for monkfish. This is the recipe of Pascal Renaud, the chef of restaurant Lou Marquès in the Hotel Jules César in Arles. It is important to keep the liquid boiling so the water and oil emulsify.*

SERVES 4
200ml/7fl oz extra virgin olive oil
16 button mushrooms, thinly sliced
12 small onions
3 potatoes, thinly sliced
3 artichoke hearts, quartered
2 tomatoes, peeled, seeded and chopped
2 garlic cloves, thinly sliced
bouquet garni consisting of 1 sprig of
thyme, 1 bay leaf and 1 sprig of fennel

long strips of zest from 2 oranges
800g/1 ¾ lb monkfish fillet, membrane
removed and cut into 12 pieces
4 slices baguette, rubbed with garlic and
brushed with olive oil
salt and freshly ground black pepper
finely chopped flat-leaf parsley, to garnish

Pour 150ml/5fl oz of the olive oil in a large flameproof casserole and then add all of the ingredients, except the monkfish and the baguette slices. Season with salt and pepper, add 2l/3 ½ pints of water and bring to the boil over a high heat, then continue boiling for 15 minutes to infuse the liquid with the aromatics. After 10 minutes, preheat the grill to high.

Reduce the heat to simmering point, add the monkfish and continue to simmer gently for 5 minutes, until the flesh flakes easily when tested with the tip of a knife.

Meanwhile, put the baguette slices under the grill and toast on both sides.

Remove the bouquet garni and strips of orange zest from the stew. Taste and adjust the seasoning accordingly.

Divide the soup between 4 warmed, deep soup plates. Use the remaining olive oil to drizzle over each plate, then scatter the chopped parsley over the top. Serve the grilled slices of baguette separately.

NAGE DE LOUP A L'HUILE D'OLIVE

Sea Bass Poached in Olive Oil

This unusual way of cooking with olive oil comes from Jean-Pierre Michel, chef/patron at La Regalido in Fontvieille, a converted olive mill and one of Provence's prettiest restaurants. Remember that the oil is being used to poach, not fry, the fish, so it should be just warm but not bubbling. It is best to use a kitchen thermometer if you can; the temperature should be around 50°C/125°F. (Illustrated right)

SERVES 4

**500ml/16fl oz extra virgin olive oil, plus
2tbsp for sautéing the onion
1 sea bass or brill fillet, about 800g/1¾lb,
skinned and cut into 4 escalopes
1 onion, finely chopped
6 very ripe tomatoes, peeled, seeded and
very finely chopped
1tsp fresh thyme leaves
1tsp sugar
4tsp sea salt**

FOR THE VINAIGRETTE
**juice of 1 lemon
120ml/4fl oz olive oil
salt and freshly ground white pepper**

For the vinaigrette, whisk the lemon juice together with the salt and pepper in a bowl. Gradually whisk in the olive oil. Set aside.

Heat 500ml/16fl oz of the olive oil in a deep sauté pan over a gentle heat (see introduction). Add the sea bass escalopes and poach for 6-8 minutes or until the fish flakes easily, turning once. Remove from the pan using a slotted spoon, drain and keep warm.

Heat a little more oil in another pan over a medium heat and cook the onion until translucent, stirring occasionally. Do not let it brown. Stir in the tomatoes, thyme and sugar and cook over a low heat for 5-6 minutes.

Spoon the tomato mixture into the centre of 4 plates, then put a sea bass escalope on top of each. Garnish each plate with 1 teaspoon of sea salt poured to make a dome shape. Drizzle with the vinaigrette and serve.

POULET AU COUSCOUS

Chicken Couscous

Couscous is traditionally made in a couscousier, a deep pot topped with a large bowl for steaming. This recipe, however, shows you how to make couscous with more everyday kitchen equipment. (Illustrated left)

SERVES 4
3tbsp olive oil
1.5kg/3 ½ lb chicken, cut into 8 pieces, on the bone
450g/1lb couscous
1 large onion, cut into 8 sections
400g/14oz tinned or cooked chickpeas, skins rubbed off
1tsp cayenne pepper
½ tsp ground cumin
½ tsp ground cinnamon
1.5l/2 ½ pt chicken stock or water
3 artichokes hearts, quartered and chokes removed
3 tomatoes, quartered and seeded
2 courgettes, cut into 2cm/ ¾ in cubes
1 green pepper, cored, seeded and cut into 2cm/ ¾ in pieces
1 red pepper, cored, seeded and cut into 2cm/ ¾ in pieces

FOR THE SMEN
250g/8 ½ oz unsalted butter, diced
1tbsp coarse salt
¼ tsp **herbes de Provence**

You can make *smen* in advance and keep it chilled in a sterilized jar. Melt the butter in a small saucepan over a medium heat without letting it colour. Bring to the boil, lower the heat and simmer for 30 minutes or until the milk solids separate and drop to the bottom.

Line a tea strainer with damp muslin and sprinkle the salt and herbs into it. Carefully pour the clear liquid through the strainer into a sterilized jar. Leave to cool, then refrigerate.

Before you begin, select a large flameproof casserole or saucepan that you can fit a steamer, colander or sieve over. Heat the olive oil in the casserole or saucepan over a medium heat. Add the chicken pieces and cook them until they are brown on all sides.

Meanwhile, rinse the couscous and pour it into a large bowl. Leave to stand for 15 minutes, during which time the grains will swell. Line a large steamer or colander or sieve with damp muslin.

Add the onion, chickpeas and spices to the casserole and stir together. Pour in the stock or water. Place the steamer, colander or sieve over the casserole and pour in half the couscous through your fingers to keep the gains separate. Bring the liquid in the casserole to the boil. When steam starts to come through the coucous, add the remainder. Lower the heat and simmer, uncovered, for 30 minutes.

Remove the steamer from the casserole and skim off any fat from the chicken liquid. Add the artichokes, tomatoes, courgettes and peppers, replace the steamer over the casserole and bring back to the boil.

Lower the heat under the chicken stew and simmer for a further 30 minutes, until the vegetables are tender and the couscous is soft and fluffy. Occasionally run a fork through the couscous to keep the grains separate.

Heat 55g/2oz *smen* until melted. Spoon the couscous on to a warmed serving platter. Sprinkle with some salt and a little *smen*, working quickly and lightly running the couscous through your fingers so it doesn't become lumpy. Mound the coucous on a large platter and arrange the chicken and vegetables on top. Serve the stock separately.

CARRE ET RIS D'AGNEAU A LA TAPENADE D'OLIVES NOIRES

Rack of Lamb and Sweetbreads with Tapenade and Black Olives

An elegant dish using robust, traditional ingredients from Pascal Renaud, chef of Lou Marquès in Arles. This is not as complicated as it appears: the tapenade *and* ratatouille *can be prepared in advance and reheated while you quickly stir-fry the sweetbreads.*

SERVES 4
200g/7oz lamb sweetbreads, soaked in
water for 1-2 hours
2 racks of lamb with 8 chops each
pinch of *herbes de Provence*
salt and freshly ground black pepper
2-3tbsp groundnut oil, plus extra

FOR THE RATATOUILLE
3-4tbsp olive oil
200g/7oz courgettes, cut into 5mm/¼ in dice
200g/7oz aubergine, cut into 5mm/¼ in dice
100g/3½oz red peppers, cored, seeded and
cut into 5mm/¼ in dice
2 garlic cloves, crushed
100g/3½oz onions, chopped
pinch of *herbes de Provence*
salt and freshly ground black pepper

FOR THE TAPENADE
100g/3½oz black olives, stoned
1 hard-boiled egg, shelled and
coarsely chopped
30g/1oz capers, well drained
15g/½oz mustard
100g/3½oz extra virgin olive oil

Begin by blanching the lamb sweetbreads. It is important that they have been soaked first to remove all traces of blood. Drain the sweetbreads, then put them in a saucepan of lightly salted water and bring to the boil over a low heat. When the water boils, use a slotted spoon to lift out the sweetbreads and put them in a bowl of cold water. Remove the black veins and use your finger to rub off the thin membrane that covers them. Put them in a bowl, cover with film and set aside.

To make the *ratatouille*, heat 1 tablespoon of olive oil in a large sauté pan. Lightly fry each of the vegetables separately, adding more olive oil as necessary, then as they are done, transfer them to a large saucepan. Add the garlic, a pinch of *herbes de Provence*, salt and pepper. Stir together, then cover and keep the *ratatouille* warm over a low heat.

Preheat the oven to 250°C/475°F/gas mark 9.

To make the *tapenade*, place the olives, chopped egg, capers and mustard in a food processor and process until puréed. With the motor still running, add the olive oil in a slow stream. Transfer to a heavy-based saucepan.

Season the racks of lamb with *herbes de Provence* and salt and pepper. Brush with oil. Place them in a roasting pan and roast for 15 minutes. Remove from the oven and leave to rest in a warm place for 10 minutes. Meanwhile, deglaze the pan with 200ml/7fl oz water to make a light *jus*.

Just before you are ready to serve, heat the *tapenade* in the saucepan. Meanwhile, heat 2-3 tablespoons of groundnut oil in a frying pan and quickly stir-fry the sweetbreads.

Cover the centre of 4 warmed plates with a circle of the *tapenade* and top with *ratatouille*. Carve the racks of lamb into individual chops and arrange them, 4 to a plate, with the sweetbreads around the sides. Drizzle with the *jus* and serve.

ESTOUFFADE D'AGNEAU

Lamb Stew

Traditionally this stew was cooked slowly with the lid sealed with a flour and water paste. Today, kitchen foil is just as good.

SERVES 4
1.5kg/3½ lb leg of lamb, boned and cut into
100g/3½oz chunks
125g/4½oz onion, chopped
2 garlic cloves, lightly crushed
200g/7oz tomatoes, peeled, seeded, chopped
2tsp black peppercorns, crushed
bouquet garni of 1 sprig of thyme, 1 bay leaf,
1 sprig of parsley and a small celery stalk
1 strip orange zest, about 7.5 x 2cm/3 x ¾ in
2tbsp olive oil
1 bottle fruity red wine, such as Gigondas
200g/7oz pork belly, cut into
5 x 2cm/2 x ¾ in strips
140g/5oz pork rind, cut into 2cm/¾ in cubes
pinch of salt

Put the lamb, onion, garlic, tomatoes, peppercorns, bouquet garni and orange zest into a large casserole. Stir in the olive oil and wine and marinate for 4 hours in a cool place.

Bring a saucepan of water to the boil, then blanch the belly of pork for 5 minutes. Drain, refresh under cold water and drain again.

Preheat the oven to 180°C/350°F/gas mark 4. Stir the pork belly and rind into the casserole and season. Add enough water to cover the meat, put on the lid and cook for 20-30 minutes until bubbling. Remove from the oven, take off the lid and cover tightly with foil. Replace the lid, reduce the temperature to 120°C/250°F/gas mark ½ and cook for 3 hours until the meat is tender. Remove the bouquet garni and zest and spoon off any excess fat.

CUISSES DE LAPIN CONFITES A L'HUILE D'OLIVE

Rabbit Thighs Conserved in Olive Oil

This recipe comes from Jean-Pierre Michel of La Regalido in Fontvieille. Rabbit thighs are 'cooked' in oil in the same way as duck thighs are cooked in their fat to make a traditional confit. The time taken to prepare the rabbit thighs is long because you are letting the olive oil conserve the rabbit, not roast or braise it. Dried juniper berries can be substituted for fresh. The ideal accompaniment to this dish is mashed potatoes made with olive oil. (Illustrated above)

SERVES 4
4 rabbit thighs
75g/2 ½ oz salt
10 fresh juniper berries
2 bay leaves
3 garlic cloves, thinly sliced
4 sprigs of thyme
2 sprigs of rosemary
extra virgin olive oil

To prepare the rabbit thighs, remove any small bones but leave the main bone and truss each thigh so it will hold its shape.

Put the salt, juniper berries, 1 bay leaf and 2 sprigs of thyme in a bowl and pour in 1l/1 ¾ pints of water, stirring until the salt dissolves. Add the thighs and chill for 3 hours.

Remove the thighs from the mixture and put in a bowl of fresh cold water to cover and leave for 2 hours, changing the water several times. Remove the thighs from the water and pat dry with paper towels.

Meanwhile, preheat the oven to 180°C/350°F/gas mark 4.

Place the thighs in a deep casserole dish, pour over enough olive oil to cover and add the garlic, the remaining thyme, the bay leaf and the rosemary. Cover the casserole and cook for 20-30 minutes. Reduce the heat to 120°C/250°F/gas mark ½ and cook for 5 hours or until the flesh is tender and easily comes away from the bone.

Leave the thighs to cool. They can be left for several weeks in the oil in a cool place.

To serve, preheat the oven to 200°C/400°F/gas mark 6. Remove the thighs from the oil and roast for 20-30 minutes until all the pieces are brown.

TARTE AUX PIGNONS DE PIN

Pine Nut Tart

Pine nuts have always been ubiquitous in Provence, and have influenced many of the region's dishes. Creamy in taste and high in oil, they are expensive and normally used sparingly, as here. If expense is no object, you can use them to make the tant pour tant, *instead of the almonds. Scattered over the top of the tart, as in this recipe from Jean-Pierre Michel of La Regalido, they will brown in the oven, which brings out the best in their flavour.*

SERVES 4
1tbsp raisins
1tbsp rum
170g/6oz *tant pour tant* (equal quantities
of icing sugar and ground almonds)
150g/5 ½ oz mixed crystallized fruit,
chopped
100g/3 ½ oz butter, softened
100g/3 ½ oz pine nuts

FOR THE PASTRY
250g/8 ½ oz plain flour
115g/4oz butter, diced and softened
2 egg yolks, lightly beaten
2tbsp sugar
pinch of salt
2-3tbsp chilled water

The evening before you want to make this tart, soak the raisins in the rum in a small bowl and make the pastry.

Put the flour in a large bowl and make a well in the centre. Add all the pastry ingredients, except the water, and rub them between your fingertips until they are well blended with the flour. Stir in the water and

quickly knead into a smooth dough in the bowl, then wrap in film and chill overnight.

The next day, preheat the oven to 220°C/425°F/gas mark 7 and lightly grease a 25cm/10in tart tin with a removable bottom. Remove the pastry from the fridge and let it soften slightly.

To make the filling, use a slotted spoon to transfer the raisins to a bowl. Add the remaining ingredients, except the pine nuts, and mix together well. Set aside.

Roll out the pastry on a lightly floured surface to 6mm/¼ in thickness. Line the tin with the pastry, then trim the edge. Pour in the filling and scatter the pine nuts over the top.

Bake the tart for 10 minutes, then lower the temperature to 200°C/400°F/gas mark 6 and continue baking for 25-30 minutes, until a skewer plunged into the centre comes out clean. Leave to cool on a wire rack, then remove from the tin and serve.

GATEAU AUX CERISES

Black Cherry Cake

This cake is similar to a clafoutis*: the cherries will fall to the bottom and the cake will be quite moist in the centre. Be sure to use a light-flavoured olive oil for this, as a fruity one will taste too overpowering. You can add some grated lemon or orange zest to the mixture if you wish. (Illustrated right)*

SERVES 4
200g/7oz plain flour
2tbsp baking powder
pinch of salt
300ml/10fl oz milk
150g/5 ½ oz caster sugar
150ml/5fl oz light-flavoured extra virgin
olive oil, plus extra for greasing
1tsp vanilla essence
2 eggs
300g/10 ½ oz black cherries, stoned
zest of one small lemon or orange, grated

Preheat the oven to 180°C/350°F/gas mark 4, then oil a 20cm/8in loose-based cake tin.

Put the flour in a bowl and mix in the baking powder and salt. Make a well in the centre of the flour and gradually pour in the milk, stirring all the time, until the mixture is smooth and without any lumps.

Put the sugar, olive oil, vanilla essence and grated lemon or orange zest in another bowl, and whisk together. Gradually whisk in the eggs, one at a time. Stir in the cherries, then stir in the flour mixture until well blended.

Pour the mixture into the prepared cake tin, then bake for 30-35 minutes until a skewer inserted in the centre comes out coated with a light film of oil, but no mixture. Allow to cool in the cake tin.

RIGHT Bright blues offer casual comfort
at a café in Avignon.
RIGHT CENTRE Ochre and red-washed walls in
Roussillon mirror the surrounding soil.
FAR RIGHT Nearby vineyards echo the same warm
colour spectrum. Most of the Vaucluse,
however, is made up of garrigues: great expanses
of rugged limestone plateaux covered with
scrub, and sudden rocky outcroppings topped by
close-walled perched villages.

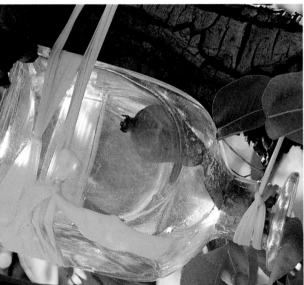

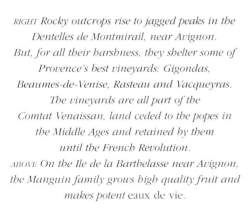

RIGHT Rocky outcrops rise to jagged peaks in the
Dentelles de Montmirail, near Avignon.
But, for all their harshness, they shelter some of
Provence's best vineyards: Gigondas,
Beaumes-de-Venise, Rasteau and Vacqueyras.
The vineyards are all part of the
Comtat Venaissan, land ceded to the popes in
the Middle Ages and retained by them
until the French Revolution.
ABOVE On the Ile de la Barthelasse near Avignon,
the Manguin family grows high quality fruit and
makes potent eaux de vie.

VAUCLUSE

'Somewhere between Vienne and Valence,' wrote the English novelist and critic, Ford Madox Ford, '... the sun is shining, and south of Valence, *Provincia Romana*, the Roman Province, lies beneath the sun. There, there is no more evil, for there the apple will not flourish and the brussels sprout will not grow at all.'

The geographical and cultural boundaries of Provence may be open to interpretation but there is no disputing its northern culinary border. It is demarcated by the olive: the great staple of the region whose oil, used as the main cooking medium, sets Provençal cuisine apart from that of the rest of France. Coming from the north by road or rail, most visitors enter Provence down the Rhône valley and will see their first olive tree just south of Valence. Almost at the same time, the landscape changes, becoming more rugged. Returning natives look for their first sight of Mont Ventoux, the signpost of Provence, and houses change from grey to gold, roofed with warm red tiles, their verandas or patios shaded by spreading plane trees. No private or public place is without its oasis of shade. 'We can always tell a northerner,' I was frequently told. 'They lie out in the sun while we seek the shade.'

Apart from a coastline, Vaucluse combines all the features of its fellow four *départements*: the mountains, gorges and high plateaux of Alpes-de-Haute-Provence and Alpes Maritimes; the wide, fertile river valleys of Bouches-du-Rhône and Var. Mont Ventoux is the first landmark of Provence, visible for miles, brooding over its surrounding *garrigue* and vineyards sloping up to villages perched on every hill. The land is limestone, rising to the heights of Mont Ventoux and to the jagged, wind-carved teeth of the Dentelles de Montmirail near Avignon. Spreading eastward is the gorge-scored Vaucluse Plateau, devoid of rivers but not short of water, for deep underground is a large network of rivers fed by Alpine snows which literally spring to the surface throughout the otherwise arid plain. The first settlers naturally built their houses around the springs, capping them with the fountains which are still at the centre of every village.

The most famous is at Fontaine-de-Vaucluse where the river Sorgue springs fully-fledged from the cliffs and becomes a swirling torrent in spring. The Romans called this valley *Vallis Clausa* (closed valley). In time, this became Vaucluse and the name was extended to cover the surrounding area.

Evidence of Roman influence is everywhere. The remains of the Roman Empire at its height are dramatic in the theatre at Orange (derived from its Celtic name, *Arausio*, and not

TRUFFLES

from the fruit) and more domestic at Vaison-la-Romaine, the most complete Roman town yet found in France. Here, apart from the first-century theatre and the second-century bridge, excavations have revealed villas, shops, gardens – even a museum.

Here there be truffles – indeed, more 'black gold' is rootled out here each year than in Périgord. Truffles, with their deep earthiness, are a world luxury but, closer to home, Vaucluse's luxury was meat. With grazing land almost non-existent, everyone hunted, relying on game for meat for the pot. By the 1970s some species faced extinction and today, quail, pheasant and even pigeons are mostly farmed. Hares are increasingly rare, except in the Lubéron and Ventoux regional parks although rabbits, being rabbits, still abound. The Provençaux do not understand our sentimentality about songbirds and there are still occasional protests about the law which now makes it illegal to sell them commercially. Some of these birds are making a tentative comeback, but they can still be shot for home consumption, usually made into pâtés like the traditional *pâté de grives* (thrush pâté).

As everywhere else in Provence, 'farmed' meat usually means sheep or goats, *gigot* of spring lamb or roasted *cabri* making little more than an annual appearance. Similarly, mutton, slow-cooked in a daube, was only occasionally served at table. Today, meat of all kinds is readily available but, like most Provençaux, the Vauclusiens still prefer animals they can breed, especially the '*agneau du soleil*', lamb from the Lubéron Regional Park which has its own *appellation contrôlée*.

PICODONS AND PICHOLINES

Far more important than the meat of the goats and sheep was their milk, drunk instead of cows' and made into simple, fresh cheeses: *chèvre* (goats' milk cheese), or *brebis* (ewes' milk cheese). The best known, Picodon, is a *chèvre*, made from 'the poor man's cow' and named for its piquant taste which comes partly from the goats' diet of wild herbs. Those made in the Drôme and around Valréas in Vaucluse have boasted their own *appellation contrôlée* since 1983, although not all Picodons meet these standards. The cheeses are made in discs, about 8cm/3in in diameter, and can be sold fresh or with a golden crust which comes from washing the cheese regularly with white wine and maturing it for a month. It has to be said that the fresh Picodons taste much like young *chèvres* anywhere. As always, it is the maturing process that gives the cheese its character. Mature Picodons are aged as winter approaches, and stored in terracotta pots to be eaten during the winter months, when the goats' milk naturally dries up.

Left-over goats' cheese is still sometimes made into *lou cachat*. Using a little blue cheese as a 'starter', the cheeses are kneaded together with pepper and *eau de vie* and allowed to ferment to the consistency of runny Brie. There the comparison stops. *Lou cachat* is overpoweringly strong and best for its medicinal properties: it's an instant sinus clearer.

Nyons, although geographically in Drôme, is the commercial centre of Vaucluse's olive groves. Close to their northernmost growth limit, they depend almost entirely on one variety of olive. The Tanche is a large, fleshy olive, picked when slightly over-ripe (and, therefore,

BELOW LEFT Nyons is the centre of the olive and olive oil industry in the Vaucluse.
FAR LEFT AND LEFT A large proportion of oil is made by the Nyons Co-operative but there are two other ancient mills, Ramade and Pont Roman, which are worth looking out for.
BELOW Sheep in the Lubéron have their own appellation *for their meat, 'agneau du soleil'.*
BOTTOM Picodon is a goats' cheese that can also claim an appellation contrôlée, *or quality guarantee, and should be washed in white wine and matured for a month to produce the piquancy which gave it its name.*

NOUGAT

*Montélimar is famous as the home of nougat,
but today much of it is mass-produced
using cheaper sugar instead of the
highly-flavoured local lavender or acacia honey
that gives good nougat its character.
Better to go to Sault, a pretty village in eastern
Vaucluse, where every small shop seems to sell it.
Right in the centre of the village is the shop
of André Boyer. Following in the footsteps
of his great-grandfather, M. Boyer and
his family still make nougat in the traditional
way, from local lavender honey and toasted
almonds, best imported Bourbon, vanilla,
sugar and egg whites.
Along with soft, chewy, white nougat, cooked
slowly and patiently stirred, M. Boyer
also makes hard nougat noir, cooked fast until
the honey caramelizes and darkens,
and probably closer to the original recipe than
the now much more familiar white.*

black) in December and January and reputed to be the best in Provence for eating. It is also pressed, producing a brownish-green, rich-flavoured oil. The smaller Picholine is picked green to become *olives cassées* (broken olives): the fruit is split open and soaked in water, changed daily, for over a week. The olives are drained and then cured in a herb-infused brine for several days. Unlike other parts of Provence, olives are still an important part of the local economy although here, too, the groves were devastated by frost in 1985 and the new growths are only just maturing. Beside the large Co-opérative Agricole du Nyonsais (which sells olives, olive oil, *tapenade*, honey and local wines) is a smaller museum tracing over two thousand years of the olive's vital role in Provençal life. A few hundred yards away, down what looks like a quiet suburban side street, is the Moulin Ramade and down by the river on the other side of town is the Huilerie du Pont Roman. Both make several styles of olive oil, some darker and some fruitier, all entitled to their own *appellation contrôlée*.

About two hundred metres from the Pont Roman, La Scourtinerie has been making the sisal mats, or *escourtins*, traditionally used in pressing olives since 1882. Today, however, modern machinery does not use them and most other mat-making companies have closed. But this is not so *chez* the Fert family. It was, after all, Ferdinand Fert, the founder of the business, who also invented these sisal mats – and the machinery to make them. So La Scourtinerie adapted, turning them into floor mats, dyed in deep but subtle colours, and opening a shop below the factory. They are still made using the nineteenth-century machines.

Almond blossom on the Ventoux plateau is the sign that spring has sprung. It was thanks to the almond tree, introduced by Olivier de Serre in the sixteenth century, that nougat (from *nucatus*, the Latin for nut) was 'invented' in Montélimar though nobody knows by whom (Marseille claims the distinction, too). Honey, that other vital component of nougat, is the traditional Provençal sweetener. Hives are nomadic, moving with the season and the 'crop'. André Augier, based in Vaison-la-Romaine, makes floral honeys from over six hundred hives scattered around Provence (see opposite, below right). The hives, moved by lorry in a sort of apian migration, go to the Alpilles in Bouches-du-Rhône for rosemary but stay closer to home for his award-winning lavender honey.

Lavender and those wild herbs such as thyme, rosemary and the various savories which enjoy struggling for their existence, flourish all across the Vaucluse Plateau. They are used to flavour everything, either directly, stirred into dishes or indirectly, infused in oils or vinegars or thrown on wood fires or hot coals to add their aroma through smoke.

Apples, pears, peaches and apricots bring their blossoms to spring in the Rhône valley. The town of Le Barroux specializes in pink apricots though the special summer markets selling this fruit alone are sadly no more. At Avignon, the river Rhône divides around the Ile de la Barthelasse which is largely given over to orchards. Here, Philippe Manguin, his father, Henri, and uncle, Jean-Pierre, grow peaches and pears on forty hectares of land. They concentrate on 'luxury' fruit which, to command top market prices, must look as good as it tastes. Any that looks less than perfect (even though it tastes as good) they distil into *eaux de vie*. The pears become Poire Williams, similar to those made in Alsace. As something of a student of 'white alcohols', I doubted the wisdom of *eau de vie de pêches*. Mine was an instant conversion: this particular fruit brandy has a fascinating and unusual taste of its own.

TOP ROW Apple orchards march across the Durance valley producing a pointilliste *pastel landscape of blossom in spring and a rich variety of fruit in autumn.*
BELOW, LEFT MIDDLE At the Manguin family's orchard and distillery, a full-grown pear pickled in eau de vie *lies in an elegant decanter.*

LEFT It's difficult to imagine how distinctive single-flavoured honeys can taste unless you've tried one of the many varieties made by people like André Augier in Vaison-la-Romaine. The most specific to Provence is lavender, a pale, waxy honey. M. Augier has six hundred hives which he moves around Provence according to the season.
FAR LEFT La Scourtinerie in Nyons still makes the sisal mats traditionally used for pressing olives. The Fert family have cleverly turned the same nineteenth-century materials and techniques into making attractive floor mats.

TOP The highly-scented, orange-fleshed melons of Cavaillon are justly famous and found throughout local markets from late spring and throughout summer.

ABOVE Another early crop is white and green asparagus, harvested from the sandy soil along the Durance Valley in early April. Its Provençal origins are always proudly proclaimed, chalked up along with the price.

ABOVE RIGHT Although most fruit and vegetables are grown commercially using herbicides and pesticides, there is increasing demand for organically grown produce, mostly grown by smallholders who offer a mixed bag of local specialities such as cardoons.

GREEN FINGERS

Lettuce was first introduced to France at Avignon, the seeds imported from Italy by the popes. The Durance valley was one of the first areas of France to be irrigated in the sixteenth century. Today, on this richly-fertile plain, relative newcomers such as tomatoes have become an important crop and *primeur* vegetables of all kinds flourish. Cavaillon has its small, highly-perfumed, orange-fleshed melons, famous for over two centuries and the year's first white and green asparagus comes from the Durance valley every April. Alexandre Dumas *père* who, apart from his many novels, wrote a *Grand Dictionnaire de Cuisine*, loved Cavaillon melons so much that, in 1864, he struck a deal with the mayor of Cavaillon, exchanging a set of his complete works (several hundred books) for a yearly delivery of one dozen melons.

Over half the melons grown in France come from this area though they are not the same variety which brought Cavaillon its early fame. The present crop are smaller with lighter green skins and darker orange flesh. They start appearing in local markets as early as April, but these early fruit are grown under plastic and lack the intense perfume and flavour of the summer crop which benefits from the unrelenting heat of the sun.

Auguste Escoffier, the great Provençal chef, was not as lucky as Dumas. During a visit to Mérindol, he suggested that as well as growing white asparagus, the farmers should grow green asparagus (even then preferred by the English) and export it to him in London. They could make a good profit, he said. Over the following years, they followed his advice and

reaped the rewards but Escoffier did not receive even one stalk of asparagus in thanks. Today, that early green asparagus, known as *asperge de Lauris* (Mérindol's next-door village), is also the gourmet's choice in France.

Cavaillon is surrounded by the Marché d'Intérêt National, France's largest 'designated market'; mile upon mile of market gardens which provide a profusion of early spring vegetables and, a summer speciality, small fresh bulbs of the white garlic so essential to Provençal cooking. The town is also the wholesale distribution centre for all Vaucluse's fruit and vegetables giving it, it is said, the highest per capita income in France.

Nearby is the Sunday morning market at L'Isle-sur-la-Sorgue. Here the river Sorgue splits into five branches and canals and the market spreads itself along their banks. The food stalls display all kinds of olives differently spiced, salt cod and anchovies, along with peppers, onions, lemons, herbs and, in spring, local early green and white asparagus, tiny violet artichokes and salad greens. But L'Isle-sur-la-Sorgue is also famous for antiques: it is the most important antique centre in France after Paris. The shops stock serious stuff but there's plenty of *brocante* and bric-à-brac out on the streets on market day. Old fish knives and forks, bundles of unmatched silver spoons, old baskets and modern *faïence* (decorated earthenware or porcelain) are eminently collectible.

Carpentras, fifteen kilometres north of L'Isle-sur-la-Sorgue, has a Friday market which threads its way through all the streets of the old town, a typical country market writ large. Stalls are packed with the freshest local produce, all of it conjuring up the colours of its season: summer pinks, oranges and reds in melons, strawberries, peaches, cherries and

TOP ROW The antiques market at L'Isle-sur-la-Sorgue features pieces serious enough to attract interior decorators from Provence and beyond. It is, however, a treasure trove of bric à brac, where enamelled coffee pots jostle with old soda syphons and chipped green-glazed earthenware.
ABOVE Market stalls stretch up and down the shaded banks of the river Sorgue. For centuries the water power was harnessed by a series of great water wheels which powered textile, paper, grain and oil mills. These industries have now gone, leaving a peaceful enclave and the remaining half a dozen wheels turning lazily, if at all.

BELOW For centuries, Avignon has been a graceful northern entrance to the warmth of Provence. From the fourteenth century, when it became a refuge for the popes exiled from Rome, until the present day, with its thriving annual Dramatic Arts Festival, it has been a cosmopolitan centre of culture.
RIGHT Avignon is also an important commercial and industrial centre but these modern intrusions are kept away from the ancient city, its encircling ramparts and small, café-rimmed squares. Within its walls, Avignon boasts the great Palace of the Popes and the twelfth-century bridge of Saint-Bénézet, which today stops abruptly half-way across the Rhône.

PAIN BEAUCAIRE

There is still a strong tradition of breadmaking kept alive in various parts of Provence. In Sarrians, Marius Dumas still bakes his bread in a three-hundred-year-old wood-burning oven behind a tiny shop. He has taught the Japanese how to make French bread, but his great specialities are both regional: pain Beaucaire, *a time-consuming loaf made by rolling and folding a soft dough as if it were puff pastry. Unlike most bread, it is not left to double in size before baking and produces a dense-textured, soft loaf.* Pain au coings *is an autumn and winter treat made by wrapping bread dough around halved, peeled quinces and baking until the fruits soften.*
Not far away at Le Barroux, monks at the Monastère Sainte-Madeleine bake and sell miches *(large round white loaves), olive bread and* demi-seigle aux noix, *studded with walnuts.*

tomatoes; the greens of spring in young asparagus, baby lettuce and spinach; the fresh green and white of *blettes* (Swiss chard), and young leeks; autumnal shades of gold and russet in grapes, apples, pears and pumpkins, *tresses*, or plaits, of bronze shallots; even winter is evoked in the greyish-silver of the thistle-like cardoon, the paper whiteness of strings of now-dry garlic, the smooth pale brown of potatoes, the purple-green of cabbages and the violet-tinged oval tips of artichokes.

An expensive winter souvenir might be a fresh truffle bought from one of a handful of dealers who appear between November and March. A much cheaper year-round one is a pretty tin filled with *berlingots*, the barley-sugar-like boiled sweets created for a banquet given by Pope Clement V. Very ordinary in themselves, they are yet another example of nothing ever going to waste. As the story goes, the pope's chef had some sugar syrup and caramel left over from an intricate *pièce montée*. Combining the two produced little sticks of candy which were broken up and passed among the guests.

The power of the medieval Church of Rome still exudes from the Papal Palace in Avignon and, across the river Rhône at Villeneuve-les-Avignon, there are still the mansions of cardinals and other courtiers who followed Pope Clement V when he fled from Rome in the fourteenth century. The Holy See already owned most of the rich Vaucluse plain in the form of an old county called the Comtat Venaissan, named after its original capital Venasque, and over the next century, his successors bought Avignon and added more land, until it amounted to almost all the territory that constitutes Vaucluse today. Even after the papacy returned to Rome, it held on to its Provençal property: the Comtat Venaissin only becoming part of France during the French Revolution.

Avignon itself is a bustling, friendly city, still surrounded by ramparts although only about half the famous bridge, built in 1190, remains, stretching part way across the Rhône. Avignon manages to combine modernity with history and culture in a most satisfying and lively way, not least at its annual summer festival of the dramatic arts. The best view of Avignon is from across the river, especially at sunset, where you can look back over the water to see the pale ramparts topped by higgledy-piggledy red-tiled roofs, all crowned by the great cathedral and Palace of the Popes looking down from the Rocher des Doms.

VINEYARDS OF THE VATICAN

Vaucluse has by far the best wines made in Provence, thanks largely to the popes' almost century-long reign at Avignon when they came to own most of the surrounding area including the Rhône valley and the Vaucluse plateau. Here they planted vines, notably at a place called Châteauneuf-Calcernier where they built a summer residence. The wines from the surrounding slopes quickly became popular.

The appeal of the village was enhanced in the nineteenth century when a marketing-minded owner of one of the vineyards renamed it Châteauneuf-du-Pape and gave the wine credit for his continued virility in old age. Then, in 1923, another owner, Baron Le Roy, laid down the rules for its *appellation contrôlée*, or guarantee of place of origin and quality.

AIGUEBELLE LIQUEUR

The centuries-old monastic tradition of distilling herbs for medicinal purposes has produced a notable liqueur at the Abbaye de Notre Dame at Aiguebelle. Simply called Verte, *it is bright crème-de-menthe green but it is neither sticky nor oversweet.*

In 1889, Père Jean Beyssier developed a potion made from pure alcohol infused with a variety of herbs that was so strong it could only be taken a drop at a time on a sugar cube. Known as Brother John's Elixir, it soon got a local reputation as a cure-all.

In 1933, casting around for what the monks describe as their 'long tradition of finding new ways of making money', a Brother Francis suggested that, if they lowered the alcohol content and added sugar, they could sell the elixir as a liqueur.

Now bottled at forty-five per cent proof, Verte *is an infusion of up to eighty herbs and plants. Some, like verbena, mint and sage are found locally but others, such as nutmeg, cinnamon and cloves come from abroad and one, the geranium bulb, is found only in India.*

These rules became the basis for all subsequent *appellations* in France. So sure of their authority were the vineyard owners that, in 1954 when flying saucers were regularly sighted over France, they simply issued a decree forbidding them, whatever their nationality, to land in, take off from, or fly over the commune of Châteauneuf-du-Pape. Perhaps they associated their name with infallibility.

Most of the wine is red, dark, spicy and rich and can be made from thirteen different grapes, although Grenache and Syrah predominate. The whites, also rich and aromatic, deserve to be better known. After Saint-Emilion, Châteauneuf-du-Pape vines cover the second largest *appellation contrôlée* area in France and produce the largest volume of wine in the Rhône valley. The vines are grown on the former bed of the river Rhône and the wine's deep richness is due in part to the soil's thick covering of pebbles which create a microclimate by absorbing the sun's heat during the day and reflecting it back up to the grapes at night. Because so many varieties of grape can be used allowing almost infinite permutations, it is impossible to define the Châteauneuf taste. But the best wines will be powerful, fruity, sometimes peppery and age well for a decade or more. These wines are wonderful with lamb, not surprisingly. A visual quality clue to look for is the papal mitre and crossed keys embossed on the bottle.

Not to be sniffed at, however, is its near-neighbour, Gigondas, again made mainly with Grenache and also a fruity, sometimes peppery and long-lasting wine (see opposite). Vacqueyras ('the great wine from a little village in Provence') produces sturdy, good-value reds as well. Beaumes-de-Venise, another next-door neighbour, is well known for its *vin doux naturel*, a slightly fortified sweet white wine made from muscat grapes. We know it as a fashionable dessert wine. The French, however, drink it chilled as an aperitif. At Domaine de Durban, one of seven *domaines* making this wine, Madame Leydier told me that they would also serve it with melon, foie gras or Roquefort but never with pudding.

North up the Rhône, around Grignan, is the small Coteaux du Tricastin whose full-bodied reds are excellent when young: in fact, Coteaux du Tricastin makes a good *primeur*. Further north still, because a liking for its wines led one of the Avignon popes, John XXII, to buy the land in the fourteenth century, growers in the Valréas enclave have the right to call their Côtes du Rhône, Enclave des Papes. Seventeen *domaines* have this right for their red wines and can display an escutcheon similar to that of Châteauneuf-du-Pape.

In the south, there is the Côtes du Lubéron, awarded its *appellation contrôlée* only in 1988 but now making good – and improving – country reds and whites. So, too, is Côtes du Ventoux, made from grapes grown on south slopes of Mont Ventoux. Across the Rhône are the neighbouring villages of Lirac, now getting something of a reputation for its red wines as well as for its rosés, and Tavel, the most serious of rosés; dry, full-bodied and higher in alcohol than most.

Visitors who want to learn about, as well as taste, the region's wine can do so from the vantage point of a grand medieval chateau overlooking the Drôme-Vaucluse border. The Ecole de Vin at Suze-la-Rousse is mainly for professionals working on the scientific side of wine-making, but they also run a series of reasonably-priced two to three day courses for interested amateurs which include visits to Rhône vineyards.

CHATEAU DE SAINT-COSME

The foothills of the picturesque Dentelles de Montmirail are dotted with villages giving their names to good Côtes-du-Rhone wines, none of them anything like as well known as Châteauneuf-du-Pape. The red wines of Gigondas are often compared with Châteauneuf-du-Pape while costing less because they are not so well known. Gigondas sits in an exceptionally sunny pocket at the southern end of the Dentelles and has been known for its wine since the time of Pliny.

One man who intends to raise the profile of Gigondas is Louis Barroul, who took over the vineyards at Château de Saint-Cosme from his father in 1992. Until then, the wine produced from the fifteen hectares of vineyards was sold in bulk to a negociant. Young Louis, who went to business school as well as learning about wine as he grew up, saw a marketing opportunity in his inheritance and its history. The land of Saint-Cosme was first planted with vines in 1416 and has been in his family since 1491. The

cellars, where the wine is matured for four years in oak casks, are among the oldest in Provence and virtually unchanged from when they were built in Gallo-Roman times. The tasting room, open daily, boasts a second-century A. D. Roman vat carved out of one wall. The twelfth-century chapel of Saint-Cosme, from which the vineyard takes its name, is a tiny, restored gem in the middle of the vines, some of which are one hundred years old.

The wine, made from Grenache, Syrah, Cinsault and Mourvèdre grapes, ages well, gaining tannin and backbone from its four years in oak. It is strong and full-bodied, with a hint of blackcurrant and violets. The 1989 I tasted was rich, fruity and, according to Louis Barroul, such a good vintage that some had been bottled in magnums. The 1991 and 1992 vintages were not good but 1993 was excellent.

So far, the fifty thousand bottles made each year are mostly sold locally. But Louis Barroul is already marketing the name across France and planning an export campaign. Proud of his heritage, he is determined to put Saint-Cosme firmly on the world wine map.

HOSTELLERIE DE CRILLON-LE-BRAVE

PLACE EGLISE, 84410 CRILLON-LE-BRAVE, TEL 90 65 61 61

Crillon-le-Brave is a tiny hilltop town near Carpentras, surrounded by the vineyards of the Côtes du Rhône and Ventoux. Until 1988, it was as unremarkable as its neighbours – except for a giant bronze statue of local boy and Renaissance hero, General Crillon (whose name was later taken by that epitome of grand luxe, *the Hotel Crillon in Paris). That year, however, a young Canadian named Peter Chittick bought the local chateau and restored it into one of the most charming of small hotels. Decorated with pretty Provençal country antiques, bright Souleaido prints and deep earth tones of terracotta and ochre, it is just as* luxe *in its way as its Parisian namesake but happily nowhere near so* grand. *Mr Chittick has since bought several village houses so guests can now choose between a full-service hotel and self-catering. Whichever they choose, it makes sense to eat in the hotel's cool, arched dining room for, being a marketing man and not a chef, Chittick hired Philippe Monti to cook. For M. Monti, Crillon is like coming home (he was born in the neighbouring village of Bedoin) after working in the kitchens of no fewer than four three-star Michelin restaurants in France and a spell at Chewton Glen, one of Britain's top country house hotels.*

GALETTE D'EPEAUTRE AU CAVIAR D'AUBERGINE ET COULIS DE POIVRON

Einkorn and Aubergine Pancake with Red Pepper Sauce

Farmers around Sault, not far from Crillon-le-Brave, have once again begun to cultivate einkorn, a once almost-forgotten wheat even to the point of building their own processing plant. Pearl barley is a good substitute. (Illustrated left)

SERVES 4
**100g/3 ½ oz einkorn or pearl barley,
well rinsed**
8g/¼ oz plain flour
1 aubergine, halved lengthways
1tbsp olive oil, plus extra for brushing

1 onion, finely chopped
1 garlic clove, very finely chopped
**1 red pepper, skinned, seeded and
roughly chopped**
3-4tbsp single cream
salt and freshly ground black pepper
fresh herbs, to garnish

Preheat the oven to 180°C/350°F/gas mark 4.

Put the einkorn or pearl barley in a large saucepan and cover with twice its volume of cold water. Place over a high heat and bring to the boil, uncovered, then cover tightly, lower the heat and cook for about 40 minutes until the grains are swollen. Turn off the heat and leave the pan covered for 10 minutes, then drain. Transfer to a bowl, leave to cool, then stir in the flour.

Place the aubergine halves, cut sides up, on a baking sheet, brush with oil and place in the oven for 30 minutes or until the flesh is soft.

Meanwhile, heat the olive oil in a saucepan, lower the heat, add the onion and garlic and cover and cook until the onion is soft.

When the aubergine flesh is soft, remove from the oven and scoop out the flesh, then add it to the onion and continue cooking for 30 minutes, stirring occasionally.

To make the red pepper sauce, put the pepper in a food processor and process until it becomes a fine purée. Pour into a saucepan and heat but do not boil. Add just enough cream to make a smooth, but not thin, consistency. Season to taste with salt and pepper. Set aside and keep warm.

Lightly oil a baking sheet and 4 crumpet rings of about 9cm/3 ½ in diameter. Place the rings on the sheet. Fill each ring with a layer of einkorn, then a thin layer of the aubergine mixture and finally another layer of einkorn. Press down firmly, then carefully lift off the crumpet rings.

Preheat the oven to 180°C/350°F/gas mark 4. Place a large, lightly oiled frying pan with an ovenproof handle over a medium heat, and slide some galettes into it. Cook until the undersides are lightly browned, then put the pan in the oven for about 5 minutes. Carefully turn the galettes over and cook for another 5 minutes to lightly brown the other side. Remove the galettes from the frying pan and keep warm until all are of them are cooked. Place each galette on to the middle of a warm plate and pour the hot sauce around. Garnish with fresh herbs and serve immediately.

CRESPEOU

Layered Omelette 'Cake'

This multi-layered 'cake' is made by stacking omelettes with different fillings on top of each other. You can experiment with other colourful ingredients to use as fillings. (Illustrated right)

SERVES 4
25g/¾oz butter
2 onions, finely chopped
sprig of fresh thyme, finely chopped
12 eggs
1 red pepper, peeled, cored, seeded and finely chopped
200g/7oz black or green olives, stoned, very well drained and finely chopped
1 bunch flat-leaf parsley, finely chopped
1 bunch basil, finely chopped
salt and freshly ground black pepper

Preheat the oven to 190°C/375°F/gas mark 5 and cover a baking sheet with foil.

Melt the butter in a saucepan, lower the heat, add the onions and a little thyme and cover and cook until the onions are soft.

Break 3 eggs into each of 4 bowls and whisk lightly. Season with salt and pepper. Add the red pepper, the onions, the olives, and the chopped parsley and basil respectively to the 4 separate bowls.

In a non-stick omelette pan, make 8 omelettes, each time using half the egg mixture from each of the 4 bowls. Cook them over a high heat for one minute, so they are still runny.

Stack the omelettes on top of each other on the foil-covered baking sheet. Alternate the fillings to make a colourful layered look when the 'cake' is cut. Flip the last omelette in the pan and place it upside-down on top to give a more finished look.

Place the omelette stack in the oven for 15 minutes. Remove from the oven and let it stand for at least 15 minutes, then trim any rough edges with a knife. Serve warm or cool.

SOUPE D' EPEAUTRE

Einkorn Soup

Epeautre *(or einkorn as it is, rather Germanically, called in English)* used to be grown around the town of Sault (see recipe on page 56). This thick, wholesome soup can also be made with pearl barley, which needs slightly less simmering time than épeautre.

SERVES 4
1kg/2 ¼ lb boneless shoulder of lamb, cubed into 2cm/ ¾ in pieces
1 onion stuck with 4 cloves
1 garlic clove, crushed
1 celery stalk, diced
2 carrots, diced
1 white turnip, diced
250g/8 ½ oz einkorn or pearl barley
salt and freshly ground black pepper

Put the lamb and 2l/3 ½ pints of water in a large saucepan over a high heat. Bring the liquid to the boil, skimming any scum from the surface of the water.

Add the onion, garlic, celery, carrots, turnip and einkorn or barley. Season and return to the boil, then lower the heat, partly cover the pan and simmer until the lamb is tender and the einkorn is swollen. (This should take about two hours for the einkorn, slightly less for the barley.)

RAITO

Red Wine Sauce for Fish

Raïto *is the classic sauce to serve hot with grilled fish, though it also tastes very good with roast chicken.*

SERVES 4
3tbsp extra virgin olive oil
2 onions, finely chopped
1tbsp plain flour
500ml/16fl oz chicken stock
300ml/10fl oz red wine, such as Gigondas
2 garlic cloves, finely chopped
2tbsp tomato passata
bouquet garni consisting of 1 sprig of thyme, 1 bay leaf and 1 sprig of fennel
1tbsp capers, drained, roughly chopped
10 black olives, stoned, roughly chopped

Heat the oil in a saucepan over a medium heat. Add the onions and cook, stirring occasionally, until soft and lightly browned. Stir in the flour and cook for 2-3 minutes, then stir in 150ml/5fl oz of the chicken stock and continue cooking, stirring constantly, until thickened. Stir in the remaining chicken stock, the red wine, garlic, passata and bouquet garni. Bring to the boil and continue cooking over a high heat, uncovered, until the sauce is reduced by half.

Lower the heat, stir in the capers and olives and simmer until warmed through. Serve with grilled or poached fish.

SALADE DE PIGEON A LA FLEUR DE LAVANDE

Pigeon Salad in Lavender Vinaigrette

These days, plump pigeons for the table are farmed birds. They are a pampered breed, for it is their feed, not their particular type, which gives the birds flavour and succulence. The best will have well-rounded breasts and most chefs serve only these, using the rest of the birds and their carcasses for stock, or, as here, to make a jus as the base for a dressing. Provençal pigeons are bred to retain a gamy flavour and infusing the dressing with lavender flowers adds a delicate, contrasting flavour to the dish; it is also an unusual way of using a regional natural resource. You can increase the roasting time if you like your pigeons less pink.

SERVES 4
4-6 young, farmed pigeons, whole
300ml/10fl oz extra virgin olive oil, plus extra for brushing
1 onion, roughly chopped
1 carrot, roughly chopped
300ml/10fl oz fruity red wine, such as Côtes du Rhône
handful of lavender flowers
1tbsp good white wine vinegar
mixed salad leaves
handful of pine nuts, lightly toasted

Preheat the oven to 230°C/450°F/gas mark 8. Place the pigeons in a roasting pan, brush with olive oil and roast for 15 minutes.

Remove the pigeons from the oven and carve off the breasts, keeping each in one piece, then set aside in a warm place. Chop up the pigeon carcasses, then heat 3 tablespoons of oil in a sauté pan over a medium high heat. Add the carcasses, the onion and carrot and cook until the vegetables are brown and start to caramelize. Pour in the wine and deglaze the pan, then add the lavender flowers. Cook over a high heat until the liquid is syrupy.

Strain the liquid into a bowl and whisk in the remaining olive oil and vinegar to make a vinaigrette. Place the salad leaves in a bowl, pour over the vinaigrette and toss together.

Arrange the dressed salad leaves on 4 plates, slice the pigeon breasts into slices and arrange them alongside the salad leaves. Scatter with pine nuts and serve.

SALADE DE POMMES DE TERRE ET DE TRUFFES A L'HUILE D'OLIVES

Potato Salad with Truffles and Olive Oil

In common with many Provençaux, Guy Julien believes that truffles are peasant food and he doesn't pussyfoot around with their use. At La Beaugravière, his restaurant in Mondragon, they are used lavishly or not at all in simple, not sophisticated recipes (although you can use fewer truffles if you wish). In spite of its busy position, La Beaugravière manages to remain a tranquil haven where one can sit indoors in front of a roaring fire in winter or outdoors on the shaded patio in summer. (Illustrated left)

SERVES 4
**400g/14oz small salad potatoes such as
La Ratte, boiled in their skins
5tbsp olive oil
1tbsp white wine vinegar
55g/2oz black truffles
salt and freshly ground black pepper**

When the potatoes are cool enough to handle, peel them and thinly slice them into a bowl.

In another small bowl or measuring jug, beat the olive oil and vinegar together and season with salt and pepper. Peel the truffles and finely chop the peelings, then add these to the oil and vinegar dressing. Put the whole, peeled truffles to one side.

Add the dressing to the potatoes and gently stir together, then set aside for at least 2 hours.

Transfer the salad to a serving bowl. Use a mandolin to thinly slice the truffles over the potatoes. Season well and serve.

CARDONS BLANQUETTE

Cardoons in Anchovy Sauce

Cardoons are an edible member of the thistle family, much beloved by the Provençaux and often served as a vegetable dish at the Gros Souper on Christmas Eve. Cardoons are natives of the Mediterranean and often used, as here, as a vehicle for more robust flavours such as anchovies or Parmesan cheese. Only the inner stalks and hearts are eaten: in Provençal markets the roots, prickly leaves and stems will already have been trimmed away. If you grow them yourself, remember to do this.

SERVES 4

**1.5kg/3 ½ lb cardoons, with the
thistle-like leaves removed
juice of ½ lemon
5 garlic cloves
2 onions, quartered
bouquet garni consisting of 1 sprig of
thyme, 1 bay leaf and 1 sprig of parsley
1 small fresh red chilli, whole
4 anchovy fillets packed in oil, drained and
finely chopped
3-4 sprigs flat-leaf parsley, finely chopped
1tbsp extra virgin olive oil
1tbsp plain flour
salt and freshly ground black pepper**

Cut the cardoon stalks crossways into 2.5cm/1in strips and put them in a bowl of water with the lemon juice as you cut them. This will prevent them from discolouring.

Put 2 of the garlic cloves, the onions, bouquet garni and chilli in a large saucepan of cold water over a high heat and bring to the boil. Add the cardoons and return the water to the boil, then lower the heat and simmer for 20 minutes until the cardoons are tender.

Strain the cardoons, reserving the cooking liquid and discarding the onions, bouquet garni and chilli, then place them in a serving dish, put to one side and keep warm.

Put the anchovy fillets in a bowl and pound them down to a smooth paste with a pestle. Crush the remaining garlic cloves and add them to the bowl with the chopped parsley and mix together well.

Heat the olive oil in a small pan over a low heat, then gradually stir in the flour and cook for about 3 minutes until lightly coloured, stirring constantly. Add the anchovy paste and continue cooking over a low heat for a few minutes, stirring continuously. Stir in 300ml/10fl oz of the reserved cooking liquid and simmer over a gentle heat for 3-4 minutes, stirring occasionally, until the sauce thickens. Season with salt and freshly ground black pepper according to taste.

Pour the sauce over the cardoons in the serving dish and serve immediately.

COTES DE BLETTES AU GRATIN

Swiss Chard Ribs au Gratin

Blette *is the wide, central white rib of Swiss chard often served in Provence with a sauce as a vegetable on its own. Its ruffle of green leaves is used in soups and in the recipe for* Caillettes *(see page 123), and the leaf and rib are generally used separately.*

SERVES 4
450g/1lb Swiss chard stalks, cut into 1cm/½ in slices
200g/7oz Parmesan cheese, freshly grated

FOR THE BECHAMEL SAUCE WITH EGGS
1 onion, quartered
500ml/16fl oz whole milk
a bouquet garni consisting of 1 sprig of thyme, 1 bay leaf and a piece of celery stalk
freshly grated nutmeg
salt and cayenne pepper
60g/2oz butter, softened
60g/2oz plain flour
2 egg yolks

Bring a large pan of salted water to the boil, add the sliced Swiss chard stalks, then lower the heat and simmer for 15-20 minutes until they are tender. Drain, refresh under cold water and drain again. Transfer the chard stalks to a flame-proof shallow gratin dish and put to one side.

Meanwhile, to make the béchamel sauce with eggs, put the onion, milk and bouquet garni in a saucepan over high heat and season with a grating of nutmeg, salt and cayenne pepper. Bring to the boil, then remove from the heat, cover and leave for the flavours to infuse while you make the roux.

Melt the butter in a saucepan over medium heat, then gradually stir in the flour and cook for about 3 minutes until lightly coloured, stirring constantly.

Remove the pan from the heat and strain in the flavoured milk, stirring continuously until well blended. Stir in the egg yolks, beating them in well. Return the pan to the heat and continue stirring for 5 minutes until the sauce has thickened.

Preheat the grill to high. Spoon the béchamel sauce over the Swiss chard stalks, then sprinkle the cheese on top. Place under the grill for 4-5 minutes until heated through and well browned on top.

FILETS DE TRUITES A LA VAUCLUSIENNE

Trout Fillets, Vaucluse style

In northern Provence, until the advent of refrigeration and high-speed transport, the only fresh fish available were freshwater fish. Most trout were – and still are – caught in the rivers of Vaucluse, though they also swim in Var and Haute-Provence. Use brown trout for this recipe if you can get them, although rainbow or salmon trout can be substituted. The truffle peelings can be used to flavour neutral oil.

SERVES 4
200ml/7fl oz béchamel sauce with eggs (see previous recipe)
½ bottle dry white wine, such as Muscadet
4 trout, filleted
2 large shallots, finely chopped
300g/10½ oz white button mushrooms, finely chopped
25g/¾ oz black truffle, peeled and finely chopped (reserve the peelings)
100g/3½ oz dry breadcrumbs, for coating
light-flavoured oil, for frying

Two hours in advance, prepare the béchamel sauce, leave to cool, then cover and chill.

Put the wine in a large sauté pan or frying pan over a medium heat and bring to the simmer. Add the fillets and poach for 3-4 minutes. Remove the fillets from the pan and leave to cool, then bring the liquid to the boil and continue to boil until it is reduced by half.

Mix the shallots, mushrooms and black truffle together in a bowl, then stir in the béchamel sauce. Trim the fillets into triangles. Put the breadcrumbs in a shallow dish.

Coat the trout pieces with the mushroom mixture, then with the breadcrumbs, patting them on in even layers. Chill for 30 minutes.

Heat 1cm/½ in oil in a wide sauté pan or frying pan over a high heat until it reaches 195°C/385°F or until a small cube of dry bread browns in 20 seconds. Add the trout fillets a few pieces at a time so you don't overcrowd the pan and cook for 1 minute on each side until golden brown. Drain well on paper towels. Serve immediately with a little of the reduced poaching liquid poured over.

MELI-MELO DE LEGUMES PRINTANIERS, LANGOUSTINES ET PUREE DE PETITS POIS

Spring Vegetables and Langoustines with a Purée of Fresh Peas

This recipe is the jewel-like creation of Serge Chenet, chef of Le Prieuré Hotel in Villeneuve-les-Avignon. This fourteenth-century former priory, across the river from Avignon, is set in gardens which, though formally laid out, exude the profusion of Provence. Chef Chenet's vegetables couldn't be fresher: most are picked from the neighbours' gardens behind the tennis court.

SERVES 4

55g/2oz green beans
4 green cabbage leaves
4 baby carrots
4 baby courgettes
4 button mushrooms
4 small white onions
4 baby white turnips
1 small cauliflower, cut into florets
1 celery stalk, cut into quarters
½ fennel bulb, cut into quarters
55g/2oz butter, plus extra for tossing vegetables
white of 1 leek, finely chopped
300g/10 ½oz shelled peas
500ml/16fl oz chicken stock
150ml/5fl oz whipping cream
4 small artichoke hearts
juice of 1 lemon
1tbsp olive oil
8 large langoustines, shelled
salt and freshly ground black pepper

Bring a saucepan of water to the boil and steam the vegetables in batches, leaving out the leek, the peas and the artichokes. When tender, drain, refresh with water and cover.

Melt the butter in a saucepan, then lower the heat, add the leek and cover and cook for 2 minutes until the leek is soft but not coloured. Add the peas, cover and cook for 3-4 minutes.

Pour in the stock and continue cooking over a low heat for 20 minutes. Strain the peas and leeks into a mixing bowl and crush into a purée, then pass through a fine sieve into a dish. Whip the cream and stir into the purée, then season. Cover and set aside.

Break the stalks off the artichokes at their bases, then cut off the pointed tips of the leaves and pull them gently away from the centre. Use a small spoon to scoop out the hairy choke. Brush the cut surfaces with lemon juice to prevent them discolouring. Bring a large pan of water to a rolling boil, add the artichokes and cook at a low boil for 30-35 minutes, until tender. Remove and cover.

Heat the oil in a sauté pan, add the langoustines and quickly sauté until pink.

To serve, spread a layer of pea purée over a warmed serving platter. Place the cabbage leaves on top, then the langoustines. Arrange the other vegetables around the platter and serve at room temperature.

GRAND AIOLI

Poached Salt Cod and Vegetables with Garlic Mayonnaise

This is the great feast dish of Provence. Its components can vary but they must centre on morue *(poached salt cod) and, of course, be served with great bowls of* aïoli, *the region's classic garlic mayonnaise. (Illustrated right)*

SERVES 4

1kg/2 ¼ lb salt cod, cut from the centre of the fish
pistou (see page 121)
4 small violet artichokes, cooked *à la barigoule* (see pages 98-9)
bouquet garni consisting of 1 sprig of thyme, 1 bay leaf and 1 sprig of fennel
8 small salad potatoes, such as La Ratte, unpeeled
8 baby carrots, trimmed
300g/10 ½oz French beans
aïoli, to serve (see page 34)

The day before you want to make the recipe, put the salt cod in a large bowl, cover with cold water and leave to soak for 36 hours, changing the water every 6 hours or so.

Prepare the *aïoli*, and the *pistou* for the artichokes then cover and chill.

Two hours before the salt cod has finished soaking, prepare the artichokes as for *Artichauts Violets à la Barigoule*. Keep the artichokes and the sauce warm separately and transfer to a serving platter when the other ingredients are ready.

After the salt cod has soaked for 36 hours, remove it from the soaking liquid and drain. Discard the soaking liquid. Bring a large pan of water to the boil and add the cod and bouquet garni. Quickly bring back to the boil and cook, uncovered, at a medium boil for 15 minutes, skimming any scum that appears from the surface of the water.

Boil the potatoes and steam the carrots and beans until they are just tender. Drain well.

Drain the salt cod, skin, then cut into 8 pieces. Arrange the fish and vegetables on a serving platter, spoon the sauce for the artichokes on to another warmed serving dish, then arrange the artichokes on top. Put a bowl of *aïoli* in the centre of the table.

ROGNONS D'AGNEAU EN FEUILLES DE VIGNE

Grilled Lambs' Kidneys Wrapped in Vine Leaves

Perfect for the barbecue, these skewers are easy to prepare. Placing them about 10cm/4in above mellow coals and frequently basting them will help the vegetables caramelize, and prevent them from burning at the edges whilst staying raw in the middle. If you don't have fresh vine leaves, use tinned or vacuum-packed ones. Rinse them well and pat dry with paper towels before using. (Illustrated above)

SERVES 4

2 green peppers, deseeded
2 red peppers, deseeded
8 small shallots
2 garlic cloves, finely chopped
5tbsp olive oil
1tsp sherry vinegar
8 lambs' kidneys, halved lengthways and cores removed
16 fresh vine leaves
salt and freshly ground black pepper

Finely chop one green pepper, one red pepper and 4 of the shallots. Put these in a bowl with the garlic, olive oil and vinegar and stir together until well mixed. Season, then add the kidneys and marinate for at least 1 hour.

Cut each of the remaining peppers into 8 pieces. Put the vine leaves in a heatproof bowl, pour boiling water over them and leave for 10 minutes. Drain and pat dry.

Light the barbecue coals or preheat the grill.

Use a slotted spoon to remove the kidneys from the marinade and wrap each one in a vine leaf. Discard the vegetables used in the marinade. Thread the kidneys, and remaining peppers and shallots alternately on to 4 long skewers. Barbecue or grill, turning and basting frequently with the marinade until the vegetables start to caramelize and brown.

POULET TRUFFE ROTI

Truffled Roast Chicken

This recipe is an economical way of using truffles that still lets you benefit from their earthy flavour. Just be sure to follow the resting times given below. (Illustrated right)

SERVES 4

25-30g/ ¾-1oz black truffles
250g/8 ½ oz chicken livers, trimmed and all green parts removed
100g/3 ½ oz pork belly, diced
1 good quality, free-range chicken or *poulet de Bresse*, weighing about 1.5kg/3 ½ lb
salt and freshly ground black pepper

One day before cooking, peel the truffles and put the peelings into a food processor with the chicken livers and pork belly. Process in brief bursts until smooth, then season with salt and pepper. Transfer to a bowl, cover and chill.

At least 8 hours before cooking, thinly slice the truffles, then cut into strips about 2cm/ ¾ in long. Stir into the chicken liver mixture.

Carefully separate the skin from the chicken breasts by gently easing your fingers under the skin. Spoon in the truffle mixture and use your fingers to ease it all along the breasts. Truss the chicken, cover loosely and leave in a cool place (not the fridge) until ready to cook, so the truffle flavour permeates the flesh.

When ready to roast, preheat the oven to 200°C/400°F/gas mark 6. Wrap the chicken in foil, place in a roasting tin and roast for 1 hour. Remove from the oven, peel back the foil and roast for another 30 minutes until the breast and thighs are nicely browned and the juices run clear when the inside of the thigh is pierced with a knife. Transfer to a serving platter and leave to stand for 10 minutes.

PLATEAU A FROMAGES

A Cheeseboard

Illustrated on the tray, from left to right: Brousse du Rove; Tomme de Brebis; chèvres ranging in maturity with the freshest on the right. Illustrated at the front, from left to right: fresh chèvre bathed in olive oil, garlic and herbs; matured chèvre coated in ash; chèvre rolled in sarriette; Banon wrapped in chestnut leaves; fresh chèvre; chèvre preserved in olive oil with fresh herbs.

Provence has no real tradition of rich desserts and most meals end with fresh fruit and a cheeseboard – modest by French standards. But this was the one part of France with no dairy culture, so cows' milk cheeses were virtually unknown.

The whole of Provence makes only one-thousandth of the cows' milk cheeses of France. In the past, cheeses were made from goats' milk (*chèvres*) or ewes' milk (*brebis*) and mostly eaten fresh. Some were wrapped in cabbage or vine leaves and stored in earthenware pots to see families through the winter months when the animals' milk dried up.

Apart from *chèvres*, the other Provençal cheese speciality is *brousse*, an unsalted cheese resembling ricotta which is eaten either sprinkled with olive oil and herbs, or sweetened with sugar and orange flower water.

The sharpness of a typical *chèvre* needs the strength of character of an old-fashioned, heavy-bodied Provençal white wine, or even the contrasting sweetness of a Beaumes-de-Venise. If these wines are unavailable, it's better to steer clear of wine altogether and nibble most Provençal cheeses with fresh fruit, or with fruit preserved in alcohol for extra bite (see right for recipes).

RAISINS A L'ALCOOL

Grapes Preserved in Alcohol

The tradition of bottling fruit for winter eating is now kept alive more for pleasure than from necessity. Bottled fruit is easy to prepare and adds a bright piquancy as a dessert or to accompany cheese.

FILLS A 1 LITRE/1 ¾ PT JAR
450g/1lb white muscat grapes
500ml/16fl oz *eau de vie* or grappa
2 vanilla pods, roughly chopped
1 cinnamon stick, broken into small pieces
15 cloves
20 coriander seeds

Remove any stems from the grapes, wash them and dry carefully. Pack into a sterilized preserving jar and pour the alcohol over. Put the spices on to a square of muslin or cheesecloth and tie tightly into a bag. Add the bag to the jar, seal and leave to macerate for at least 6 months.

KUMQUATS A L'EAU DE VIE

Kumquats Preserved in Alcohol

FILLS A 1 LITRE/1 ¾ PT JAR
450g/1lb ripe but firm kumquats
500ml/16fl oz *eau de vie* or grappa
1 vanilla pod

Wash the kumquats and dry them thoroughly. Put them into a sterilized preserving jar and pour the alcohol over. Add the vanilla pod to the jar, seal and leave to macerate for at least 6 months.

RIGHT Honey is gathered from hives along the slopes of the valleys of the Var where agriculture continues as it has for centuries.

RIGHT CENTRE Medieval villages dot the landscape and most remain unspoilt, their red-tiled roofs, painted shutters and colourwashed walls gently faded by the hot sun.

FAR RIGHT These beans, displayed in a spring market, are an unusual sight to those of us more used to the shelled and dried variety.

RIGHT The Var's great tourist resort is Saint-Tropez, once a small fishing village, but, since its discovery by nineteenth-century artists, a magnet for Parisians and the summer playground of the world's glitterati. But, out of season, Saint-Tropez regains its charm and it's easy to see what first attracted painters such as Matisse and Dufy, as well as such literary figures as Colette.

ABOVE The economy of the Var depends on the vine: four-fifths of all Côtes de Provence wine comes from this département.

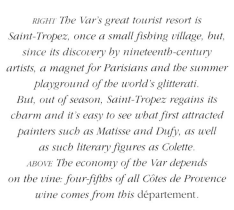

VAR

The Var is Provence's great secret; behind its long, narrow coastline, stretching from Toulon to Saint-Tropez, the land is folded in on itself, rising into parallel ranges of steep, forested hills and falling into deep, narrow gorges. This spectacular scenery is not easily accessible even today. Behind the coast road the hills of the Massif des Maures can still only be reached by narrow, twisting roads, often little more than tracks. Its northern slopes fall into the only real valley, watered by the river Argens and clad with fruit trees, vines and lavender. Then, almost immediately, the hills rise again, each topped by a small, medieval village and falling into narrow valleys of van Gogh-ian colour and beauty, a land so remote that wild boar still roam, even around the towns of Draguignan and Brignoles.

Hyères, although not quite on the sea, was the first resort along the Riviera, popular with English visitors (including Queen Victoria) before either Nice or Cannes. Indeed, it is said that the very phrase 'Côte d'Azur' was coined here. Fréjus and Saint-Raphaël claim to have been welcoming visitors since Roman times. Saint-Tropez retains its fashionability, even though it is one heaving traffic jam of vulgarity in summer. But visiting out of season, one can still see the pretty fishing port, ringed by ice-cream-coloured houses much as they looked when the avant-garde painter, Paul Signac, discovered the village and settled there in 1892. His paintings are not as well known today as those of many of his contemporaries and friends, but it was Signac who introduced Matisse, Seurat and Dufy to this part of the coast: they were inspired to a new boldness of colour in their paintings.

The small town of Le Lavandou is both resort and fishing port, and Bormes-les-Mimosas, in the hills behind, not only has spectacular views but also the restaurant of Guy Gedda, one of the great gurus of Provençal food. He opens from June to September, spending the rest of the year travelling the world as a sort of roving ambassador for Provence.

THE FRUITS OF ISOLATION

Food remains down-to-earth in the Var. On what flat land there is, along the valley of the Argens, some apples, cherries, plums and peaches are grown commercially, although the once-famous Brignole plums are now mostly grown around Digne. Market gardeners grow produce for local consumption and most households boast a fig or quince tree.

TARTE TROPEZIENNE

Tarte Tropézienne is, for me, one of the few good things about Saint-Tropez. At first sight, it looks deceptively like a simple, round sponge cake of the kind you'd find at any bring-and-buy sale. This plain-looking cake is, in fact, a soft brioche, stuffed to overflowing with a thick vanilla custard, and topped by large sugar crystals, lightly glazed. It's hard to say what makes it so extraordinarily good, except for the contrast between sight and taste. It looks heavy and over-rich, but the taste is light and not too sweet. There is the added pleasure, and almost childish delight of the rich squelch of custard that oozes from the sides as you cut into it.

Tarte Tropézienne was 'invented' by the then-owner of the patisserie, Alexandre Micka, who patented it in 1971. Other versions of this cake are generally much less lavishly filled and often substitute ground nuts for the sugar crystals.

Most of the land, however, is hillside or scrubby plateaux with very little top soil. Meat tends to come from game; as elsewhere in Provence, whole migrations of songbirds have been wiped out over the years and recent laws to protect them are still the subject of much grumbling and some demonstrating. Pigeon, however, remain unprotected, as do rabbit and hare. Roast kid is a popular, but not much less expensive, alternative to leg of lamb: restaurateurs have been known to tell foreigners that it is, in fact, a kind of lamb. Wild boar (*sanglier* is a mature beast; *marcassin* a young one) is increasingly to be found on restaurant menus throughout the Var.

The terrain and isolation of the villages means that the communities of the Var remain very much self-contained and self-sufficient. There is, of course, La Provençale, the autoroute running between the Massif des Maures and the hills of the Haut-Var from west to east, and no shortage of supermarkets, but the hilltop villages retain their completeness more than anywhere else in Provence. Few have been gentrified and there have been very few concessions to tourists. At the same time they have managed to stay in touch with the twentieth century.

Flayosc is a typical example. Perched on a hillside near Draguignan, its narrow cobbled streets, flanked by tall, close-shuttered houses, converge on a small square shaded by plane trees and with a mossy fountain at one corner. Even though the supermarkets of Draguignan, the former *département* capital, are only ten kilometres away, the Flayoscians support two butchers, three boulangeries, a *poissonnerie*, three mini-supermarkets, a wine co-operative and, keeping up with the times, a small delicatessen where fresh pasta and ravioli are made daily, and a Vietnamese takeaway. There is also L'Oustau, a restaurant with a hundred-franc menu embracing regional dishes such as daubes and *pieds et paquets* (sheep's feet and tripe) and a café/bar noted for its Saturday speciality, *paella*.

Draguignan itself is the local centre for olive oil and hosts a great international fair and olive oil competition every July. Draguignan was once the centre of a silkworm industry which gradually died out in the early years of this century. Mulberry trees are still found in many a private garden and have been hybridized with the more common plane tree to produce an attractive shade against the strong Provençal sun. Although no longer the capital

ABOVE LEFT Flayosc is typical of the unpretentious hilltop villages of the Var.
LEFT Quince orchards have mostly been left to go wild although they are harvested to make jelly or quince paste.
FAR LEFT Sweet-tasting apricots are grown in large quantities in the Var.
OPPOSITE, BELOW RIGHT Mulberries used to support a silk industry but trees are now kept for shade.
OPPOSITE, BELOW LEFT Traditional crops such as peaches are grown commercially in the orchards of the Var département.

of the *département*, Draguignan retains its prosperity, partly from the ten thousand military personnel based in Canjuers, the second largest military training ground in Europe.

West of Draguignan are some of the prettiest hilltop towns in the Var. Aups is one of the few still to rely on agriculture more than tourism and its Wednesday and Saturday market is one of the best places to buy local honey. The walled village of Lorgues hosts a vibrant Tuesday market, popular with foreign residents and visitors. It forms a link in a pretty necklace that includes two totally unspoilt villages: Cotignac, tucked under sheer cliffs and Entrecasteaux, dominated by a seventeeth-century castle. The major town in this chain is Salernes, where no fewer than fifteen firms manufacture tiles from the area's naturally-coloured clays, in shades from palest beige to deep terracotta.

GUIEU HONEY

With flavours as diverse as lavender, lime, sunflower, chestnut and pine, the mono-floral honeys of the Guieu family are famous throughout France. The family has made honey here for over a century. The honey is made in hives moved all over Provence according to the seasonal flowerings (Vaucluse for lavender, Haute-Provence for pine). This apian migration is done by lorry, and 'renting' a farmer's field or orchard is usually paid for with a modest amount of honey: the farmer, of course, also needs the bees. The honey-filled frames are brought back to Les Ruchers du Bessillon, the Guieu headquarters and shop in Cotignac. The shop and store are lined with clearly-labelled pots and drums of honey, for the flavour of each variety is quite distinct. Rather like wine, each year's harvest will be slightly different depending on the weather and the intensity of flowering.

OPPOSITE BELOW The main street of Cotignac is shaded by plane trees and watered by the trickle of moss-covered fountains so typical of all Provence's villages. In summer, the village is lively with an open-air carnival. The rest of the year, it dozes gracefully in the sun.

FAR LEFT These goats' cheeses are on display at Lorgues, one of the liveliest of markets in the region and a favourite of the many foreigners who have retired to the area. The stallholders play up to this a little, but it is still fun to visit and the quality of produce is high. Every village has its weekly market with near-neighbours choosing different days of the week so that the same traders can visit each in turn.

LEFT ABOVE This fougasse-shaped bread is sliced to take various fillings: it is a phenomenon which seems to be unique to Lorgues.

LEFT BELOW Spices at Lorgues market make a colourful display.

BELOW Each village has its own wine co-operative where you can take your five-litre 'cubi' to be filled with the local red, white or rosé for just a few francs a litre.

WINES OF THE VAR

Prosperity in the Var comes from wine: four-fifths of all Côtes de Provence comes from this region. Sixty per cent of the wine is rosé, which, perhaps it should be said, is not a mixture of red and white wine blended together but is made from red grapes in one of two ways. In the first, after pressing, the skins are left with the juice to ferment, until they have dyed it the right colour. In the second, the juice is coloured by the crushing of the skins during pressing and before fermentation, producing a light salmon colour which the French call *gris* and the Americans 'blush'.

Vines have grown on these slopes since 600 B.C., producing wines mentioned favourably by Julius Caesar, and from the Middle Ages until the Revolution they were much drunk by the French court. In this century, however, the reputation of Provençal wine in general, and rosé in particular, has been low, dismissed as high-priced 'plonk'. Now, however, winemakers are mobilizing and modernizing, realizing that with a little thought and effort, they can produce clean, fresh wines at reasonable prices. Many of these wines are reds, but there are also much-improved rosés and whites.

RIGHT *The vines of the Var have, until recently, been much better known for their quantity than their quality. Indeed, it is difficult to produce a sophisticated wine in a climate so hot that alcohol levels are naturally high. Reds, in particular, suffered from this headache-inducing quality and only a few pioneers tried to experiment, mostly by importing cooler-climate grape varieties. One success story was at Château Vignelaure in the northern Var, where Georges Brunet brought his experience as owner of a Bordeaux chateau to bear. Brunet is no longer the owner of Vignelaure, but the wine still lives up to the reputation he achieved for it.*

How lucky they are, the grapes of Vignelaure, to be nursed in the sun and made into such elegant wine — Fill your glass and taste Provence.

Peter Mayle

THIS CHÂTEAU VIGNELAURE VINTAGE IS PRESENTED BY THE
WRITER PETER MAYLE AND THE DESIGNER ALAN FLETCHER

Standards were set out in an *appellation contrôlée* in 1977 and the best wines are now awarded a seal of approval by its trade association, the Confrérie des Enchanteleurs des Côtes de Provence, a brotherhood which has taken as its motto the somewhat punning '*in vino veritas, in vino severitas*', which would loosely translate as, 'in wine there is truth, in wine there must be rigorously applied standards'.

The majority of really good Côtes de Provence wines have been created by individual winemakers during the last twenty years or so, most of them concentrating on reds. But there have been wines entitled to call themselves *crus classés* since the 1940s, much to the annoyance of some of Bordeaux's top producers who resent the appearance of the same words that denote top quality in Médoc on the labels of what they regard as comparatively inferior wines.

In Provence, twenty-three wines can bear this label and, says André Garnoux, the president of the syndicate that controls the Côtes de Provence *appellation*, more now deserve it. Expansion is legally barred but Etienne Matton, owner of Château Minuty at Gassin, near Saint-Tropez, and rightly proud of his wines, is leading a ginger group of fifteen fellow producers in an attempt to change the rules.

Up in the north, on the plateau of the Haut-Var near Rians, Georges Brunet, who once owned Château La Lagune in Bordeaux, created Château Vignelaure based on Cabernet and Syrah grapes. He also introduced the Lafite Rothschild tradition of different artist-designed labels for each vintage, adding a quotation from a distinguished writer. The quality of these span from Anthony Burgess, who considered himself as much a composer as an author and composed a few bars of music for the 1980 label to the words of the author Peter Mayle on the 1989 label: 'How lucky they are, the grapes of Vignelaure, to be nursed in the sun and made into such elegant wine. Fill your glass and taste Provence' (see left, below). M. Brunet sold the vineyard in 1986, but the wines continue to be made with care and in the traditional Bordeaux style.

Some of Provence's wines have always kept their good reputations as wines of high quality. Bandol, from the hillsides around Toulon, produces a strong, spicy, tannic red that can age well, along with a number of good dry whites and rosés. Inland, around Vidauban, Domaine des Féraud was one of the first vineyards to experiment with Syrah and Cabernet Sauvignon grapes, traditionally the backbones of Rhône and Médoc wines respectively.

Only eighteen thousand hectares of vines in the Var are embraced by the *appellation contrôlée*. The vast majority of the vines produce Côteaux Varois, of varying quality but improved enough to be recently given the status of VDQS (*Vins Délimités de Qualité Supérieure*; this indicates a wine good enough for quality control but not yet up to *appellation contrôlée* standards) or *Vin du Pays* (a rank created to encourage southern French wine makers to try harder). Both types of wine are good value, especially if bought in the region itself from local co-operatives. Visitors should try to visit La Maison des Vins Côtes de Provence, just outside the town of Les Arcs-sur-Argens, where tutored tastings are   regularly held and where the restaurant earns praise from *Gault et Millau*, the top French food guide.

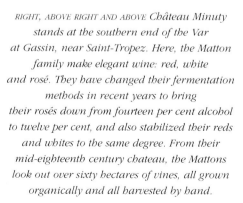

RIGHT, ABOVE RIGHT AND ABOVE Château Minuty
*stands at the southern end of the Var
at Gassin, near Saint-Tropez. Here, the Matton
family make elegant wine: red, white
and rosé. They have changed their fermentation
methods in recent years to bring
their rosés down from fourteen per cent alcohol
to twelve per cent, and also stabilized their reds
and whites to the same degree. From their
mid-eighteenth century chateau, the Mattons
look out over sixty hectares of vines, all grown
organically and all harvested by hand.*

PAWLOWSKI

*Henri Pawlowski is a shining example of the
new generation of wine makers who are
determined to raise the quality and reputation
of Côtes de Provence wines. In 1975, the
Pawlowskis bought twenty-seven hectares of
garrigue between les Arcs-sur-Argens and
Vidauban, and Henri went back to school to
learn winemaking. Over the next ten years, the
scrubland was gradually cleared and planted
with 'noble' grape varieties such as Cabernet
Sauvignon, Syrah and Mourvèdre, as well
as traditional varieties such as Cinsault.
The new vineyard, named Domaine des Hauts
de Saint-Jean, produced its first small vintage in
1977. Henri Pawlowski was one of the first
winemakers in the area to concentrate
on making red wine. Today, sixty per cent is red,
including a Cuvée Spéciale Père Henri, a
blend of Cabernet Sauvignon and Syrah grapes
and described by the prestigious French
Hachette wine guide as 'very harmonious,
powerful and persistent.' This wine regularly
wins gold medals at wine fairs, as does the small
quantity of white Pawlowski makes.*

OLIVES AND OLIVE OIL

*The olive is the signature of Provençal cooking.
One of the most ancient of symbols,
the olive branch is a sign of peace throughout
the world; it was an olive branch that
a dove brought back to Noah as proof that Man
could return to earth and dry land.
Olive oil has always been the cooking medium of
Provence although recent years have
seen it become fashionable all over the western
hemisphere, wherever the 'Mediterranean
diet' is promoted for health. Even though it
produces only a tiny proportion of the
world's olive oil (less than 0.02 per cent), this
has been good news for Provence
where the majority of olive groves were
devastated by frost in 1985. The trees didn't die
but the frosts killed them off above ground
and new shoots take ten to fifteen years to
mature. Many olive trees were abandoned but
now demand is increasing and they are
starting to be tended once more.
The olives which thrive in Provence
are many and varied: Aglandau, Cailletier,
Lucques, Menzanille, Picholine, Royale,
Salonenque, Tanche, Violette, and more. All
olives will be green if picked unripe;
black if left until ripened. Harvesting begins
in September for green olives and runs
between November and February for black
ones. So far no mechanical method of
harvesting has been developed, so the
age-old sight of men and women
on ladders knocking olives on to nets
spread on the ground below is an autumnal
feature all over Provence.
Nyons, in the north of Provence, is
famous for Tanches, the only olive with an
appellation contrôlée. These olives
are plump, black and acknowledged as the
best table olive. When ripe and black,*

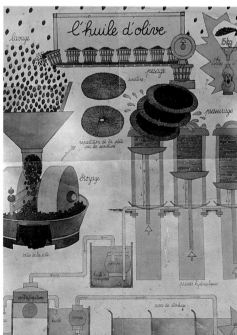

the fruit is pressed to make a deep green, heavy oil, best for using 'raw' in salad dressings. Mausanne is the centre for the oil of La Vallée des Baux, the most fashionable oil among chefs. It is made from a variety of olives which are picked unripe, and the oil is lighter and less assertive than many.

Around Nice, the small, wrinkled, black Cailletier is essential to salade niçoise, pissaladière and to accompany any aperitif. Pressed by small mills like Alziari and Moulin de la Brague, it produces a gentle but fruity oil. In the Lubéron, and near Draguignan, and in Haute-Provence, the variety of olives includes the Aglandau, which stays dark green when ripe and produces a robust oil.

Almost all olives will be sold to local mills, either to be cured, to eat whole or to be pressed into oil. This process is explained, very charmingly, by the poster displayed at Moulin Cornille in Mausanne (far left, below). The fruit is crushed by stone wheels as at the Pont Roman mill in Nyons (left, below) until it forms a smooth paste. Traditionally, the paste is then spread on scourtins, (woven hemp mats) and pressed to release a mixture of oil, water and some solids. The oil is then separated from these in a centrifuge.

This traditional way of pressing is known as cold-pressed. A harsher method would heat the paste and change the taste of the oil. The best oils will always be cold-pressed but they will also be graded into categories:

extra virgin olive oil: 1 per cent or less acidity
fine virgin olive oil: 1-1.5 per cent acidity
semi-fine virgin oil: 1.5-3 per cent acidity

You don't have to be a food snob to keep two or three different kinds of oil on hand: a robust oil for sprinkling on breads; a medium oil for salads or sautéing; and a light oil for delicate food such as fish.

LA TABLE DU MARCHE

38 RUE CLEMENCEAU, 83990 SAINT-TROPEZ, TEL 94 97 85 20

Christophe Leroy is a young chef building his reputation in Saint-Tropez, a town where it's all too easy to pander – at exorbitant prices – to the undiscriminating tastebuds of the glitterati who flock there each summer. But M. Leroy will none of that: he is building a small empire based on excellence. La Table du Marché is on one of the narrow streets winding up from the old port, a haven of peace only yards from the harbourside cafés crammed with the 'see and be seen by' crowd. It is a busy bistro with, on the floor above, La Salle à Manger, a more formal restaurant. Originally from Normandy, M. Leroy is a convert to Provence and his cooking is substantial and based on the best of ingredients. Above the kitchen is a gleaming stainless-steel bakery where he produces patisserie for both restaurants and, the latest string to his bow, a delicatessen, also called La Table du Marché, just a few doors away.

PETITS FARCIS DE LEGUMES AUX SENTEURS DE PROVENCE

Stuffed Baby Vegetables with Tomato Coulis

SERVES 4
4 tomatoes
4 baby aubergines
4 courgettes
4 onions
**300ml/10fl oz olive oil, plus extra
for drizzling**
4 large, open-cap mushrooms
4 garlic cloves, crushed
15g/ ½ oz belly of pork, finely chopped
150g/5 ½ oz fresh breadcrumbs
200g/7oz Parmesan cheese, freshly grated
**100g/3 ½ oz veal escalope, lightly grilled and
finely chopped**
75g/2 ½ oz fresh basil, finely chopped
salt and freshly ground black pepper
100g/3 ½ oz rocket, to garnish

FOR THE TOMATO COULIS
300g/10 ½ oz tomatoes, peeled and seeded
100ml/3 ½ fl oz olive oil
salt and freshly ground black pepper

Cut a 'hat' off the top of each tomato, then hollow them out and set aside the tops and insides. Salt the insides of the tomatoes and set them aside to drain, upside down, for 1 hour.

Preheat the oven to 190°C/375°F/gas mark 5. Slice a 'hat' lengthways off the top of each aubergine and each courgette, then hollow them out and set aside the tops and insides. Slice a 'hat' off each onion and carefully remove the centres, putting the tops and centres aside.

Place the aubergines and tomatoes on a baking sheet, brush with a little of the olive oil and roast for 20 minutes. Remove the vegetables and set aside. Increase the oven temperature to 220°C/425°F/gas mark 7.

Separately blanch the courgettes and mushrooms for 3-4 minutes, and the onions for 10 minutes. Drain, refresh under cold water and drain again. Set aside.

Meanwhile, to make the stuffing, put all the scooped-out flesh and the garlic in a food

GENDARME DE SAINT-TROPEZ

Chocolate Policeman's Hat

(Illustrated right)

SERVES 8
FOR THE FILLING
500ml/16fl oz double cream
1 vanilla pod, split lengthways
125g/4 ½ oz sugar
5 egg yolks

FOR THE CHOCOLATE MOUSSE
100ml/3 ½ fl oz double cream
200g/7oz top quality plain chocolate
50g/2oz butter, softened
300ml/10 ½ fl oz whipping cream

FOR THE BASE
400g/14oz top quality plain chocolate

processor and process until smooth. Put the remaining olive oil in a saucepan over medium heat, then add the vegetable purée and the belly of pork and heat through, stirring until well blended.

Remove from the heat and set aside until cool. Stir in the breadcrumbs, Parmesan cheese, veal and basil. Season and blend well.

Oil a baking tray, then stuff each of the vegetables and put a 'hat' on each. Place on the baking tray, drizzle with a little extra olive oil and cook for 30 minutes, until tender.

To make the tomato *coulis*, purée the tomatoes in a food processor. With the motor running, steadily pour in the oil and season.

To serve, spread a little of the *coulis* on each of 4 plates, then top with one each of all the vegetables. Garnish with rocket and serve.

Make the filling at least 6 hours before serving. Put the cream and vanilla pod into a saucepan. Bring to the boil, then remove from the heat.

Whisk the sugar and egg yolks until the mixture thickens and becomes pale yellow. Gradually whisk in half the cream, then the other half at once and return to the pan. Heat gently until the custard thickens. Do not boil.

Remove from the heat and strain into a clean bowl. Cover the custard suface with cling film and leave to cool to room temperature. Refrigerate for 6 hours.

To make the mousse, bring the cream to the boil in a saucepan for 1 minute, then set aside.

Roughly chop the chocolate and melt in a bain marie or saucepan fitted over a pan of hot water. When the cream is lukewarm, pour it on the chocolate and whisk. Leave to cool.

In a large bowl, whisk the butter for 2-3 minutes until it turns pale. Still whisking, slowly add the chocolate cream until smooth. Whip the cream, then fold into the mousse.

Melt the 400g/14oz chocolate as above and spread it out on a cold baking sheet to 6mm/¼in thickness. Once it has set, use a biscuit cutter to cut 12 circles of about 10cm/4in diameter. Place one circle on each of 8 dessert plates. Spoon the mousse around the edge of the chocolate circles to make a ring with walls 4.5cm/1½in thick. Spoon the chilled custard into the centre of each ring and cover with a layer of the mousse. Using a palette knife, smooth down the top and sides.

Cut the last 4 circles in half and arrange one under each mousse to resemble the peak of the gendarme's cap. Chill before serving.

SOUPE DE POISSONS DES ROCHES

Rockfish Soup

There are many versions of this classic but it will be made most successfully if you have access to the fresh rockfish sold on market stalls in Provence. These will include tiny rascasse and small crustacea such as favouilles, a shore crab found nowhere else. You can substitute non-oily white fish such as bream, mullet or John Dory for these rockfish. I've suggested you use a mouli-légumes; you can, of course, use a food processor but you will lose some texture. (Illustrated above)

SERVES 6-8
100ml/3 ½ fl oz olive oil
200g/7oz onions, finely sliced
**1kg/2 ¼ lb Mediterranean rockfish,
cleaned and left whole**
**200g/7oz conger eel, cleaned and chopped
into bite-sized chunks**
1 garlic head, halved crossways
3 very ripe tomatoes, chopped
**bouquet garni consisting of thyme, bay leaf,
sprig of fennel**
50ml/3tbsp Cognac
pinch of saffron
salt and freshly ground black pepper
1 baguette, sliced and toasted, to serve
***rouille* (see page 34), to serve**

Prepare the *rouille* and set aside. Heat the oil in a large saucepan over a medium heat. Lower the heat, add the onions, cover and cook until they are translucent. Raise the heat and let the onions brown.

Over a high heat, stir in the fish, garlic, tomatoes, bouquet garni and Cognac and cook for 5 minutes, stirring occasionally.

Pour in 1.5l/2 ½ pints water, bring to the boil, and cook, uncovered, for 20 minutes.

Remove the bouquet garni and purée the soup in batches either through the coarse blade of a mouli-légumes or a processor. Strain into a saucepan. Stir in the saffron and season. Bring to the boil, then simmer for 5 minutes. Serve with the baguette and *rouille*.

ANCHOIADE

Anchovy Paste

Use as a dip for crudités or to top toasted baguette slices. A little added to both fish and meat stews is the 'mystery' ingredient of many a secret recipe. (Illustrated right)

SERVES 4
2 garlic cloves
20 anchovy fillets tinned in oil
5tbsp extra virgin olive oil
1tbsp white wine vinegar
1 egg yolk

Put the garlic cloves in a food processor and chop very finely. Add the anchovies and process again.

With the motor running, add 1 tablespoon of the olive oil, the vinegar and the egg yolk through the feed tube. With the motor still running, add the remaining olive oil in a slow, steady stream through the feed tube. Serve immediately or cover and chill until required.

FLAN DE LOTTE

Monkfish Flan

This flan has no pastry; instead its container is a shallow porcelain dish with 'ears', usually called an egg dish or cocotte. Individual gratin dishes covered with kitchen foil can also be used as containers.

SERVES 4
300ml/10fl oz dry white wine, such as Chardonnay
450g/1lb monkfish fillet, with its membrane removed
2 tbsp extra virgin olive oil
3 tomatoes, peeled, seeded and chopped
4 eggs, lightly beaten
55g/2oz butter
salt and freshly ground black pepper

Preheat the oven to 150°C/300°F/gas mark 2.

Put the white wine and 200ml/7fl oz of water in a large sauté pan or frying pan and bring to simmering point. Add the monkfish fillet and poach for 15 minutes until the flesh flakes easily when tested with the tip of a sharp knife. Remove the monkfish from the poaching liquid and drain well on paper towels. Skin the monkfish carefully and flake the fish into a bowl. Put to one side.

Gently heat the olive oil in a saucepan. Add the tomatoes and cook over a low heat, stirring occasionally, until soft. Stir into the monkfish, then stir in the beaten eggs and season with salt and pepper, according to taste. Spoon into 4 well-buttered, individual cocottes. Top each one with a knob of butter.

Line the bottom of a deep ovenproof dish with newspaper, then add the cocottes. Pour in enough boiling water to come halfway up the sides. This method creates the effect of a bain-marie and prevents the cocottes from coming into contact with the dish. Put the dish in the oven and cook for 30 minutes until the flans are set. Leave to cool completely, then chill. Serve cold as a summer starter.

RAVIOLES DE CHEVRE

Pasta Stuffed with Goats' Cheese
(Illustrated left)

SERVES 6
3 crottins soft goats' cheese, each one sliced
in half to make 6 flat discs
4 tomatoes, peeled, quartered and seeded

FOR THE PASTA
550g/1 ¼ lb plain flour
4 eggs
3tbsp red wine vinegar
pinch of salt

FOR THE VINAIGRETTE
100ml/3 ½ fl oz olive oil
2tbsp white wine vinegar
leaves from 3 sprigs of fresh thyme
salt and freshly ground black pepper

With your hands, combine the flour, eggs, vinegar and salt in a bowl to a soft dough.

Knead the pasta and roll out as thinly as you can on a lightly floured work surface. Leave the pasta to dry for one hour. Cut the pasta into 12 squares or circles large enough to leave a margin of 2 ½ cm/1in when the cheese is placed in the centre of the pasta shape.

Put one cheese slice on half the pasta shapes, then cover each with a second pasta shape, dampen the edges with a little water and press to seal. Cover and chill.

Place the vinegar, thyme and seasoning into a bowl and gradually whisk in the olive oil.

Arrange the tomatoes on a platter and lightly coat with half the vinaigrette. Bring a large pan of water to the boil, add salt, then the pasta and cook for 3 minutes or until *al dente*. Drain well and place on top of the tomatoes. Drizzle the remaining vinaigrette over the pasta.

PAPETON D'AUBERGINES ET TOMATES CONFITES

Aubergine Mousse with Tomatoes Confites

This is an elegant version of a dish which is found in many Provençal homes and on most menus. Sometimes the mousse is served on its own with toasted baguettes and a dollop of tomato purée. Alternatively it can be presented as quenelles, *as in this recipe. However you decide to present this dish, tomato is an essential accompaniment. (Illustrated right)*

SERVES 4

3 aubergines
5 tbsp olive oil, plus extra for brushing the aubergines
6 ripe, firm tomatoes, peeled
15g/ ½ oz butter
1 large onion, finely chopped
2 garlic cloves, finely chopped
2tbsp fresh thyme leaves
2tbsp crème fraîche
1tbsp good red wine vinegar
salt and freshly ground black pepper
chervil or chives, to garnish

Preheat the oven to 150°C/300°F/gas mark 2.

Cut the aubergines in half lengthways, then place them, cut sides up, on a baking tray and brush them evenly with olive oil. Put in the oven and bake for 30 minutes or until the aubergines are soft.

Meanwhile, cut 3 of the tomatoes into quarters and remove the seeds, then place in one layer in a lightly-oiled ovenproof dish. Finely chop the remaining tomatoes and set aside. Melt the butter with 1 tablespoon of olive oil in a large saucepan over a medium heat, then lower the heat, add the onion and garlic and cover and cook until the onion is translucent, but do not let it brown.

Remove the aubergines from the oven and raise the temperature to 220°C/425°F/gas mark 7.

Scoop the aubergine flesh out of the shells and chop it finely. Add the aubergine and thyme to the onion and season with salt and pepper. Add the chopped tomatoes to the onions and stir together well. Stir in the crème fraîche and adjust the seasoning. Cook for about 5 minutes, stirring occasionally.

Use 2 soup spoons to form the mixture into 12 small *quenelles* and place them on a warmed serving platter.

Place the tomato quarters in the hot oven for 1 minute, remove them, then arrange them on the platter in a circle, alternating them with the aubergine *quenelles*. Gently flatten the tomatoes with a fork to resemble petals.

Mix 3-4 tablespoons of the olive oil with the red wine vinegar and salt and pepper to form a vinaigrette. Spoon the vinaigrette evenly over the *quenelles* and tomatoes and decorate with chervil or finely chopped chives.

SALADE DE ROUGETS A LA TAPENADE

Red Mullet Salad with Tapenade

SERVES 4

4 red mullet fillets
3tbsp olive oil, plus extra
***tapenade* (see page 98 for ingredients)**
6 radishes, sliced
6 spring onions, sliced into rings
handful of *mesclun* or mixed salad greens
8 slices baguette, toasted
4tsp sherry vinegar
salt and freshly ground black pepper
extra olive oil, for pan frying

Brush the red mullet fillets with 1 tablespoon of the olive oil, season with salt and pepper and set aside in a cool place for 15 minutes.

To make the *tapenade*, place all the ingredients except for the olive oil in a food processor and process until puréed. With the motor still running, add the olive oil in a slow stream. Set aside.

Bring a small saucepan of salted water to the boil, then blanch the radishes and spring onions for 1 minute. Drain, refresh under cold water and drain again. Set aside to cool.

Arrange the salad leaves on 4 plates and scatter the radishes and spring onions around. Spread the *tapenade* on the baguette slices and add 2 slices to each plate. Whisk 2 tablespoons of oil with 3 teaspoons of vinegar, add salt and pepper, then pour over the salad.

Heat a little olive oil in a large sauté pan or frying pan over a high heat. Add the red mullet fillets and pan-fry for 1 minute on each side. Transfer the fillets to the plates. Whisk the remaining 1 teaspoon of vinegar and 1 tablespoon of water into the cooking juices, then pour over the fish. Serve immediately.

SALADE DE POISSON CRU MARINE AUX HERBES FRAICHES

Salad of Raw Fish Marinated with Fresh Herbs

The fish for this dish must be ultra-fresh. Do not prepare in advance, or the lemon juice will start to 'cook' the fish.

SERVES 4

400g/14oz sea bass or sea bream fillets, skinned and thinly sliced

FOR THE DRESSING

400ml/14fl oz extra virgin olive oil
100ml/3 ½ fl oz lemon juice
1tbsp finely chopped fresh tarragon
1tbsp finely chopped fresh basil
pinch of ground ginger
pinch of cayenne pepper
salt and freshly ground black pepper

FOR THE GARNISH

100g/3 ½ oz French beans, topped and tailed
2 tinned artichoke hearts, drained and halved
2 tomatoes, peeled, seeded and diced
fresh chervil

Top and tail the beans and then steam them for five minutes. Whisk all of the dressing ingredients together in a bowl. Add the fish slices and quickly turn them in the dressing to coat, then remove them and leave to drain in a nylon sieve.

Mound the beans on a serving platter, then arrange the artichoke hearts and the fish slices around. Scatter with the diced tomatoes and decorate with chervil.

BRANDADE DE MORUE

Salt Cod Beaten with Olive Oil and Garlic

Nîmes claims brandade de morue as its own but it is popular all over Provence. You can make this in a food processor but be very careful that you don't over-process it into a gluey mess. It must retain some texture and should end up homogenous and white. Serve with boiled potatoes.

SERVES 4

800g/1 ¾ lb salt cod, sawn into 3 or 4 chunks
300-400ml/10-14fl oz extra virgin olive oil
200-250ml/7-8fl oz milk
2 garlic cloves, crushed
2-3tbsp double cream
freshly ground black pepper
freshly grated nutmeg

A day and a half in advance, put the salt cod in a large bowl, cover with cold water and leave to soak for 36 hours, changing the water every 6 hours.

Remove the salt cod from the soaking liquid and put into a deep saucepan. Add enough fresh water to cover and slowly bring to the boil, then cook at a medium boil for 15 minutes, skimming the surface occasionally.

Meanwhile, heat the olive oil and milk in separate pans without letting the milk boil.

Drain the salt cod and when cool enough to handle remove the skin and flake the flesh into a large bowl. Add the garlic and beat together with a wooden spoon. Continue beating and add the olive oil and milk in steady streams. Beat in just enough double cream to make the mixture smooth, silky and white. Season with pepper and nutmeg. Serve immediately.

SEICHE A LA PROVENCALE

Cuttlefish, Provençal Style

I have adapted this recipe from the original for octopus, the father bear of the cephalopod family. You can use this or squid, the mother bear. Baby bear, or cuttlefish, are not so easily found away from the Mediterranean. There are only two ways to cook this family: either very fast or very slowly – anything in between will prove tough. (Illustrated above)

SERVES 4

1kg/2 ¼ lb cuttlefish, ink sac and bone removed, tentacles cut off and reserved
100ml/3 ½ fl oz olive oil
1 onion, finely chopped
3 tomatoes, peeled and finely chopped
350ml/12fl oz dry white wine
350ml/12fl oz boiling water
bouquet garni consisting of thyme, bay leaf and a sprig of fennel
2 garlic cloves, finely chopped
handful of parsley, finely chopped
salt and freshly ground black pepper

Wash the cuttlefish thoroughly under cold running water, pat dry and cut the body into 2cm/¾in rings, and then the tentacles to 2-3cm/¾-1¼in lengths.

Heat the oil in a casserole and lightly brown the onion. Add the cuttlefish and tomatoes. Stir well, bring to a simmer and add the wine and the boiling water.

Season with salt and pepper, add the bouquet garni, cover the casserole and cook over a low heat for 2 hours, or until the cuttlefish is tender.

Add the garlic and parsley and serve.

GIGOT EN POT POURRI A LA PROVENCALE ET AUX TRUFFES

Braised Leg of Lamb Stuffed with Garlic and Truffles

Pot-pourri is the Provençal term for an aromatic mixture of vegetables, here intensified with truffles. (Illustrated opposite)

SERVES 4
55g/2oz black truffles
10 garlic cloves, finely chopped
1 leg of lamb, about 1kg/2 ¼ lb, boned
100g/3 ½ oz lard
4 onions, thinly sliced
5 carrots, thinly sliced
5 small white turnips
350ml/12fl oz rosé wine
a bouquet garni consisting of 1 sprig of thyme, 1 bay leaf and 1 sprig of fennel
olive oil
1 green pepper, cored, seeded and diced
1 aubergine, diced
4 tomatoes, peeled, seeded and diced
salt and freshly ground black pepper

Finely chop 15g/½ oz of the truffles, then mix with half the chopped garlic. Put this mixture in the pocket left by the bone in the lamb, then tie the opening closed with kitchen string.

Melt the lard in a flameproof casserole large enough to hold the lamb. Add the lamb and brown it on all sides, then remove it and add the onions, carrots and turnips. Cook over a medium heat, stirring often until they are brown, then return the lamb to the casserole.

Pour in 650ml/24fl oz of water and the wine. Add the remaining garlic and bouquet garni, season and bring to the simmer. Cover the casserole, lower the heat and simmer for 45 minutes, occasionally turning over the lamb.

Heat a little olive oil in a frying pan over a high heat. Stir-fry the pepper, aubergine and tomatoes, each separately, until they start to colour, adding more oil as necessary. Add to the casserole.

Remove the lamb and leave to rest for 15 minutes. Transfer the vegetables to a serving platter, slice the lamb and place on the vegetables. Grate the truffles over the meat.

CABRI ROTI AVEC DE L'AIL ET DES POMMES DE TERRE

Roast Kid with Garlic and Potatoes

Kid is a good alternative to gigot of lamb for an Easter feast. You can buy kid from a Turkish, Greek or Middle-Eastern butcher's shop.

SERVES 4
1kg/2 ¼ lb Maris Piper potatoes, sliced
1 garlic head, sliced in half crossways
1 leg of kid, about 1.5kg/3 ½ lb
groundnut oil, for brushing
1 bunch flat-leaf parsley, finely chopped
salt and freshly ground black pepper

Preheat the oven to 180°C/350°F/gas mark 4 and lightly oil a large ovenproof dish.

Strew the potatoes in the dish, then put the garlic, cut side up, in the centre. Season the kid, brush with groundnut oil and place the kid, skin side up, on the garlic and strew with parsley. Cover with kitchen foil and roast for 1 hour. Remove the foil and roast for 20 minutes.

Transfer the kid to a warmed serving platter and leave to rest for 10 minutes. Cut each garlic half in half again and serve with the kid.

DAUBE DE SANGLIER

Wild Boar Stew

Boar still roam the wooded hillsides around Draguignan, so chef/patron Gérard Werts, of La Roche Aiguille in Ampus, has no trouble getting supplies. You and I will have to use the farmed animal, which takes less time to cook.

SERVES 4
1kg/2 ¼ lb wild boar, cut into 2.5cm/1in cubes
100g/3 ½ oz bacon, rind removed and diced
4 shallots, finely chopped
4 garlic cloves, finely chopped
2 onions, thinly sliced
500ml/16fl oz Côtes de Provence
2tbsp olive oil
bouquet garni consisting of 1 sprig of thyme, 1 bay leaf and 1 sprig of fennel
zest of 1 orange, cut into long strips
2tbsp tomato purée
2tbsp plain flour
salt and freshly ground black pepper

Put the boar, bacon, shallots, garlic and onions in a bowl and pour over the wine. Leave to marinate for 4 hours, stirring occasionally.

Strain, reserving the wine, and pat dry.

Heat the olive oil in a large flameproof casserole over a medium-high heat. Add the marinated ingredients and cook, stirring occasionally, until they brown. Add the bouquet garni, orange zest and tomato purée, stir well and cook for 1 minute.

Stir in the flour and cook for 2-3 minutes. Pour in the reserved wine and season, then simmer until the sauce thickens. Cover, lower the heat and cook for 3 hours, adding water if necessary, until the meat is tender and the sauce is glossy and dark. Serve with pasta.

SAUCISSONS DE FIGUES

Fig 'Sausages'

Figs, both fresh and dried, are an ancient fruit in Provence. This is a recipe from the Draguignan chapter of the Académie Nationale de Cuisine. The recipe was created in 1990 after the members' successful attempt at the record for the world's longest sausage. Having no charcuterie of their own, the members decided to use a product they were known for: figs. Measuring almost 165 metres, and weighing 260 kilograms, their sausage beat the previous record holder by almost 45 metres. They are rather good cut into slices and served with vanilla ice-cream or crème fraîche, but they can also be served whole to accompany duck or game.

SERVES 4
1kg/2 ¼ lb dried but moist figs, with hard bits trimmed off
150g/5 ½ oz butter
4tbsp set honey
550g/1 ¼ lb walnuts, blanched almonds or skinned hazelnuts
4tsp candied orange peel, finely chopped
icing sugar, for dusting

Put half the figs in a processor with half the butter and 2 tablespoons of honey and process until finely chopped. With the motor running, add half the nuts through the feed tube and process until coarsely chopped. Add 2 teaspoons of orange peel. Remove the mixture and repeat with the remaining ingredients.

Dust the work surface with icing sugar. Divide the mixture into 8 portions and, using your hands, roll each into a sausage shape. Wrap each 'sausage' in cling film and chill for at least 3 hours.

BLANCMANGER AUX AMANDES

Almond Blancmange

This is an old-fashioned, soothing dessert with a subtle almond flavour. (Illustrated opposite)

SERVES 4
1 ½ sachets of gelatine
250g/8 ½ oz blanched almonds
150ml/5fl oz milk
250g/8 ½ oz sugar
500ml/16fl oz whipping cream

Pour 2-3 tablespoons of water into a saucepan, add the gelatine and soak for 5 minutes. Set over a low heat and shake the pan gently until the gelatine dissolves.

Put the almonds in a food processor and process, adding 150ml/5fl oz of water a little at a time through the feed tube. With the motor running, pour in the milk all at once and process until the mixture is smooth.

Put the almond-flavoured milk in a saucepan with the sugar and heat over a medium heat, stirring constantly, until the sugar dissolves. Do not let the milk boil.

Strain the mixture through a fine sieve lined with muslin, into a clean pan. Wring out the muslin to extract all the milk. Place the pan over a low heat, add the dissolved gelatine and stir. Remove any skin that forms and leave the milk to cool to lukewarm.

Whip the cream until stiff peaks form, then stir it gently but thoroughly into the almond milk. Pour into a mould or individual serving bowls and refrigerate for one hour, or until set.

If the blancmange was made in the mould, dip it very quickly in hot water, then put a serving plate on top and invert the mould and plate, giving a sharp shake half-way over.

RIGHT AND CENTRE The limestone plateaux of the Alpes-de-Haute-Provence are deeply scored by narrow gorges and pierced by sheer cliffs. Life has always been hard and food basic but good, with staples such as these country breads. Goats are one of the few beasts able to survive the harsh conditions.

FAR RIGHT Santons (terracotta figures which decorate the Christmas crib) wear costumes that hark back to a not-too-distant past.

RIGHT Spring turns these harsh plateaux into drifts of silvery purple as mile upon mile of lavender bushes breaks into leaf and then flower. These fields (which look like an invasion of hedgehogs after the harvest in July or August) extend well into the Vaucluse. However, Digne is the acknowledged lavender capital and host to a great fair every August.

ABOVE In the west of the département, around Sisteron, wheat and barley fields are bright with summer-flowering poppies.

ALPES-DE-HAUTE-PROVENCE

When Napoleon escaped from Elba, he made his dash for Paris from Golfe Juan in the Alpes Maritimes straight through Château-Arnoux, along the road now called the route Napoléon. Château-Arnoux was then, as it is now, a great crossroads in the mountains and plateaux that make up most of Alpes-de-Haute-Provence where the road from Grenoble to Marseille meets the road from Avignon to Nice.

Forty kilometres north is Sisteron, where the valley cut by the river Durance narrows. The only gateway from the north to this part of Provence, it was heavily fortified by the Romans and marks a dramatic change of countryside from the dairy pastures of the Dauphiné region. The olive trees start at Laragne-Montéglin, about twenty kilometres north of Sisteron. Lavender clothes the slopes purple in summer, silver-grey in winter; soil and roof tiles become terracotta; with the perfume of wild herbs, they all signal Provence.

This is the country of local writer Jean Giono, who, in the years between the two World Wars, wrote movingly of the destruction of rural life and the advent of industrialization in this, the most remote part of Provence. Most of us know Giono's work through its adaptation into some fine films by Marcel Pagnol, who tends to take a rosier view of the subject matter than its author. When Pagnol turned to writing in the late 1940s, he wrote a trilogy of childhood reminiscences whose warmth and romanticism are in sharp contrast to Giono's tone of underlying pessimism. Giono describes how whole villages were emptied of their populations in the rush to factories and cities. Some, like Redortiers near Banon, remain abandoned even today.

Others, like Forcalquier or Manosque, reached their peak of power and importance in the twelfth century. Forcalquier became part of Provence in 1209, and for the next century was the capital of Haute-Provence and a great cultural, political and economic centre. Today, it is a quiet market town of some four thousand souls and little remains of its former grandeur.

Manosque retains its medieval heart and surrounding plain of orchards. But its position, in the Durance valley at the eastern end of the Lubéron mountains, makes it a natural crossroads between Avignon, Marseille and the main route north that has brought it the autoroute, power stations and a nuclear research centre. The rest of the region has a geography so forbidding that I doubt any more roads have been built since Napoleon's day.

The Durance cuts up the western side of the *département*, with steep mountains rising to its west and, to its east, an area of high, isolated plateaux. A series of peaks and gorges rises

WIND-DRIED AND
SALT COD

*Before refrigeration and modern transport
methods, stockfish or wind-dried cod
(above left) and salt cod (above right) were two
of the few regular sources of protein
available in the remote inland parts of
Provence. Both ancient preserving methods,
they are easy to tell apart. Stockfish looks
like old shoe leather; salt cod is more
appetizing and glistening with salt crystals.
Cod is not a Mediterranean fish, but
was first brought south by Vikings to trade for
olive oil and wine. Both wind-dried
and salt cod need long soaking times. The flaky,
white fish is either served whole to
become the centrepiece of a Grand Aïoli
(see page 62) or it is pounded with olive oil to
become* brandade de morue. *No one knows the
origin of* brandade *although similar dishes
are found along the Spanish and Portuguese
coastline and even around Venice. The first
written recipe dates to the end of the eighteenth
century but its author, Grimod de la Reynière,
steadfastly refused to reveal its source.*

and falls with tiny, isolated villages perched improbably on the top of every hill or clinging in steep tiers to its sides. Part of the southern boundary twists along the spectacular Grand Canyon du Verdon, the deepest gorge in Europe with sheer drops of over six hundred metres in places (and to which the 1990s have brought bungee-jumping). Where there are plateaux, most of the land is *garrigue*, rocky scrub covered with wild herbs: thyme, oregano, bay, rosemary, mint, lavender, juniper and *sarriette*. In summer especially, the air is literally perfumed with their fragrance.

This part of Provence was so isolated, so sparsely populated and so poor that many butchers plied their trade only at Christmas and Easter. Yet this land supports one of France's most famous meats: Sisteron lamb, given its specific flavour by the herbs and mountain grasses on which it grazes (see opposite). Apart from the sheep and goats kept for milk and cheese, animal husbandry is unknown. Instead, anything that moved was shot, so much so that wild game is now rare and even pigeons are being farmed for the table. *Pâté de Grives* (thrush pâté) was the great regional delicacy – until song birds were banned for commercial use. This has not prevented them from being shot, however: the law still allows them to be cooked and eaten in the privacy of your own home. But larger game is so scarce that sometimes a solitary rabbit or pheasant will be the only bag on a cold winter's day spent trekking, accompanied by dogs, over a scrub-covered hillside. Even a good day will only produce a modest meal for the pot.

But a natural lack of plenty does not mean you eat badly. In reality, the situation is quite the reverse: when your resources are limited you give what you do have great care and attention. Today, this is exemplified by the Gleizes, *père et fils*, at La Bonne Etape Restaurant in Château-Arnoux (see page 97). Over the past thirty years, Pierre, and now his son, Jany, have built up a wide network of local suppliers and cultivated a hotel herb and vegetable garden of distinction. Here you can trust that the Sisteron lamb and Banon cheese (which the Gleizes' mature themselves) are the genuine article. Even Parisians make special journeys to Château-Arnoux just to eat La Bonne Etape's Provençal specialities which include duck with lavender honey and rabbit with hyssop, as well as more modern dishes such as stuffed courgette flowers.

*LEFT AND OPPOSITE BELOW The making of
thrush pâté (pâté de grives) was once
a thriving local industry but
now the shooting of songbirds has
been banned for commercial use:
restaurants can no longer offer it on
their menus nor companies produce it
for sale. One sympathizes with the
birds, but also with peasants trying to
scratch a living out of bare cliffs and
rugged terrain where only a few
gnarled olive trees grow.*

LEFT AND ABOVE The town of Sisteron gives its name to the breed of lamb whose meat is given added savour by the wild herbs it grazes on.

SISTERON LAMB

Sisteron lamb served at La Bonne Etape restaurant in Château-Arnoux (see page 97) is the single best beast of its kind I have ever tasted. Like most people, I suspect, I had put its reputation for excellence down to the fact that it grazes not on grass but on the pungent wild rosemary and thyme of the garrigue around the fortress-town of Sisteron. That, of course, is part of it, but the Sisteron is a specific breed. It is a small but very stocky pré-Alpe du Sud, rather than a kind of merino, like its rivals, the Alpille (from the mountain chain of that name between Avignon and Arles) and 'agneau du soleil' lambs from the Lubéron. Strictly speaking, it is not a lamb when it is slaughtered although the small size of the joints may make us think so. Because the breed is so small, with flesh concentrated in its haunches, the Sisteron is not butchered until it is one hundred and twenty days old or more, giving greater depth of flavour and texture to the meat.

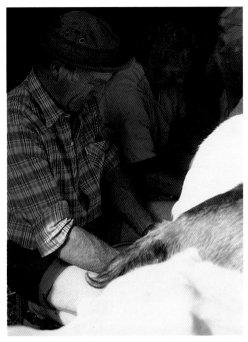

BANON CHEESE

Banon is a goats' or sheep's milk cheese, traditionally made on the isolated farms
around the town of the same name in the mountains of Haute-Provence. Small plump discs
of about one hundred grams, they are matured for two to three weeks, then wrapped
in eau-de-vie-soaked chestnut leaves and aged until pungent and runny inside, with a bluish crust
on the outside. The goats' milk used to make Banon cheeses is much higher in fatty acids
than cows' milk. It is these fatty acids that give all goats' milk cheeses their particular pungency.
The sheep's milk Banon is almost extinct and the goats' milk one is rare. Most Banon cheeses,
even from local markets, are now made of cow's milk from the Dauphiné.
Banon is one of the very few Provençal cheeses made to mature well (most sheep's and
goats' milk cheeses are best eaten fresh and when young). It is worth seeking
out the real thing in the markets of Banon itself and nearby Château-Arnoux. Young Banons
are sold white, sometimes wrapped in green chestnut leaves but more often coated in
dried sarriette, *the summer savory which grows on the scrubby plateaux of the*
Alpes-de-Haute-Provence. Sarriette *is also known as* Poivre d'Ane *(donkey's pepper).*
Banon cheeses are still kept in the old-fashioned way, when the objective was
to make the cheese last through winter when the sheep's and goats' milk dried up.
The cheeses were stored in sealed terracotta jars with pepper, thyme, cloves
and bay leaves and covered with eau de vie *or olive oil.*

*RIGHT This herd of elegant goats is kept by
M. and Mme Chabaud near the village of
Banon. The Chabauds are one of an
increasingly rare number of goats' milk suppliers
in Provence. They sell most of their milk to
M. Romain Ripart who makes it into a number
of different cheeses, including Banon. True
Banon cheeses are difficult to track down
far from their home ground.
One of the few reliable sources is at the Tuesday
and Saturday market in Banon itself.*

*ABOVE AND RIGHT The Chabaud's herd of goats
must be brought indoors twice a day to
be milked by hand. These elegant
creatures provide rich, whiter-than-white
milk which is much higher in fatty
acids than cows' milk.*

FROM MILK TO CHEESE

*M. and Mme Chabaud supply milk from their herd of goats to cheesemakers throughout the
region. Unfortunately, small suppliers like the Chabauds are becoming increasingly
rare in Provence. For a start, the goats need to be milked twice a day and are therefore extremely
time-consuming to keep. It seems unlikely that the younger generation will
continue a tradition that is both labour-intensive and no longer necessary (thanks to
refrigeration and freezing, cheesemakers can now buy their milk from co-operatives many miles
away and transport it over long distances). Banon cheeses made from goats' milk have
now become relatively rare. Furthermore, now that cows' milk is easily
available, it is often used in preference to goats' milk.
M. Romain Ripart makes some of the best of the area's cheeses on his smallholding just
south of Banon. He keeps his own herd of about sixty goats but their milk represents
only a small part of the one thousand five hundred litres he uses each day. The rest is bought
in from small farmers and trusted suppliers like the Chabauds. His Banon de Banon
is one of the few authentic examples of this traditional local cheese to survive. M. Ripart also
makes Bûchette de Banon. This, his own 'invention' is a small, slim, hand-rolled log
of chèvre, matured for two to three weeks but not wrapped, merely decorated with a sprig
of sarriette. His other cheese, a Tomme de Chèvre Fraîche, is a small, soft cheese, decorated with
sarriette and sold when it is only three days old.*

TOP *The capital of Alpes-de-Haute-Provence is*
Digne, a remote but vital crossroads.
It has been known from Roman times as a spa
town: hence its full name of Digne-les-Bains.
It is also in the centre of the Réserve Géologique
de Haute-Provence, the largest geological
reserve in Europe. The best way of reaching
Digne is by the Chemin de Fer de la Provence.
Nicknamed the 'Pine Cone Train',
the carriages climb over nine hundred metres
on their journey through spectacular scenery of
pine-clad mountains and narrow gorges.
ABOVE *Today, Digne is most famous as the*
lavender capital of Provence.

This reliance on making the most of what you have also comes into its own in the *Treize Desserts*, the finale of the *Gros Souper*, the meatless Christmas feast eaten before Midnight Mass everywhere in Provence. The *Treize Desserts* is an assemblage of fruits, sweetmeats and nuts arranged in little baskets around *fougasse*, the thirteen components representing Christ and his apostles (see pages 104-5). There will be both white and black nougat and, representing the four monastic orders, almonds (Carmelites), figs (Franciscans), hazelnuts (Augustines), and raisins (Dominicans). Apples, pears, clementines or mandarins, grapes, winter melon, dates, prunes, chestnuts and slices of quince jelly usually make up the numbers. These simple components are also the most common way to end any daily meal.

The land of Haute-Provence may be inhospitable but its climate boasts three hundred days of sunshine a year. The sun's strength encourages fruit and vegetables on every tiny pocket of workable earth and the large area of fertile flat land along the Durance river around Manosque is one great orchard: a sea of white and pink apple blossoms in spring.

Digne-les-Bains, a spa town as its name suggests, is the *département* capital. The town retains a quiet elegance with its thermal baths which date from Roman times. It is the centre of Provence's lavender production, celebrated with an annual fair in August. Digne is also something of a centre of culture: it is home to an annual film festival, an international sculpture symposium and a Provençal song festival, as well as a feminist film festival and the International Accordion Festival.

Digne is the northern terminus of the narrow-gauge Chemin de Fer de la Provence, a now privately-owned railway that runs to Nice and provides one of the best ways to visit some otherwise almost inaccessible mountain villages such as Annot and Entrevaux. The railway climbs over nine hundred metres on its journey between Nice and Digne. The pine forests between the two towns harbour wild boar and mushrooms. Entrevaux holds an annual mushroom conference but is better known for its extraordinary fortress built by Vauban, Louis XIV's military engineer. Sited above the small town, it is accessible only by zig-zagging ramps; a stiff half-hour walk, but worth it for the views of the Var valley.

LA BONNE ETAPE

CHEMIN DU LAC, 04160 CHATEAU-ARNOUX, TEL 92 64 00 09

Pierre Gleize and his son Jany cook some of the best and most Provençal of food in one of the most unlikely of places, isolated in the middle of Haute-Provence. But their hotel and restaurant has been an important haven for more than two centuries, situated at the major crossroads that is Château-Arnoux, where the roads from Grenoble, Marseille, Nice and Avignon meet. Virtually everything they use comes from carefully chosen local suppliers, since Gleize père et fils like to exercise a strict, though benevolent, quality control. And, as both men frequently remark, they have everything they need here naturally – except good beef and cream. 'People say cooking is lighter now,' says Jany, 'but here that's traditional. Most of our ways of cooking come from thinking about what we've got and making the most of it.'

FLEURS DE COURGETTES FARCIES, SAUCE POMME D'AMOUR

Stuffed Courgettes with a Tomato Sauce

Pommes d'amour *(literally, love apples) was the name given to tomatoes when they were introduced to France. Make sure the courgette flowers are clean by shaking them gently upside down. Do not wash them. (Illustrated right)*

SERVES 4

3 small courgettes, roughly chopped
6tbsp extra virgin olive oil
2 garlic cloves, finely chopped
6 sprigs fresh basil, finely chopped
6 sprigs fresh mint, finely chopped
24 leaves flat-leaf parsley,
finely chopped
handful of dry breadcrumbs
1 egg, lightly beaten
16 courgette flowers
250ml/8fl oz chicken stock
salt and freshly ground black pepper

FOR THE SAUCE

1.5kg/3 ½ lb ripe tomatoes, peeled, seeded
and finely chopped
120ml/4fl oz olive oil
50g/2oz each fresh basil, chives and
parsley, finely chopped
8g/ ¼ oz coriander seeds, crushed
1 garlic clove, crushed
1 lemon, peeled and cut into small cubes

Put all the sauce ingredients in a small bowl and stir together. Cover and leave in a warm place for 12 hours.

Purée the courgettes in a food processor. Heat the olive oil in a sauté pan over medium heat, then add the courgette purée and garlic. Cook for 5-6 minutes, then remove the pan from the heat, stir in the herbs and season.

When the mixture is cool, stir in the breadcrumbs and egg. Preheat the oven to 180°C/350°F/gas mark 4. Carefully stuff the flowers, gently pressing the petals around the stuffing. Arrange the stuffed flowers in a lightly-greased gratin dish, pour in the stock and drizzle with the oil. Cover with aluminium foil. Cook for 15 minutes and serve warm with the sauce.

AIGO BOULIDO

Garlic Broth

Literally 'boiled water', this soup is nothing more than water flavoured with garlic and herbs and, although it has its roots in poverty, it is also drunk for its medicinal qualities. Garlic is acknowledged worldwide for its ability to aid circulation and digestion, and for its antiseptic properties. Sage is thought by the Provençaux to calm nerves and stop asthma. Indeed, they say that the person with sage in their garden will not need a doctor. Of the soup itself, they say it saves your life. Today, this is often served as the soup course of the Gros Souper on Christmas Eve, and some people add a poached egg per person just before serving. It is always poured over rustic, country-style bread and drizzled with olive oil.

SERVES 4
4 garlic cloves, crushed
8 fresh sage leaves

4tbsp extra virgin olive oil, plus
a little extra to serve
1 egg yolk
4 slices country-style bread
100g/3 ½ oz Gruyère cheese, grated
salt and freshly ground black pepper

Put the garlic, sage leaves and olive oil in a large saucepan over a high heat. Add 2l/3 ½ pt water and bring to the boil, then cover and continue to boil rapidly for 15 minutes to allow the aromatics to infuse into the liquid. Season with salt and pepper. Strain the liquid into a clean pan and keep hot.

Put the egg yolk in a small bowl and lightly beat, then beat in 5-6 tablespoons of the hot liquid, 1 tablespoon at a time. Remove the saucepan of liquid from the heat and whisk in the egg mixture. Keep warm over a low heat but do not let the soup boil.

To serve, put a slice of bread in each of 4 warmed, deep soup plates. Drizzle with a little extra olive oil and sprinkle with the cheese, then ladle the soup over.

TAPENADE

Olive and Anchovy Dip

Everyone has their own version of tapenade, but this one comes close to being a classic. A Monsieur Meynier of the Maison Dorée in Marseille is credited with its invention. Tapenade can also be bought ready made in jars. (Illustrated left)

SERVES 4
250g/8oz black olives, stoned
100g/3 ½ oz anchovy fillets in oil, drained
100g/3 ½ oz capers, drained
sprig of thyme
1 bay leaf
2 garlic cloves
3tbsp Cognac (optional)
4tbsp extra virgin olive oil
freshly ground black pepper

Put all the ingredients apart from the olive oil in a food processor and process until a purée forms. With the motor still running, add the olive oil in a slow, steady stream. Transfer to a serving bowl and serve immediately, or cover with film and chill until required. Serve as dip with crudités, hard-boiled eggs, or spread on slices of toasted baguette.

ARTICHAUTS VIOLETS A LA BARIGOULE

Baby Artichokes, Barigoule Style

A la barigoule has two meanings in Provence, and both can apply to artichokes. It can mean, as here, braised in wine and olive oil. Or, it can mean stuffed with a local mushroom called barigoule. (Illustrated opposite)

SERVES 4

2-3tbsp *pistou* (see page 121)

12 small violet artichokes

juice of 1 lemon

100ml/3 ½ fl oz olive oil

300g/10 ½ oz white salad onions,
finely chopped

170g/6 oz young carrots, finely diced

200g/7oz tomatoes, peeled, seeded, chopped

4tbsp tomato purée

4 garlic cloves, finely chopped

100g/3 ½ oz basil leaves, finely chopped

bouquet garni consisting of 1 sprig of
thyme, 1 bay leaf and 1 sprig of fennel

200ml/7fl oz dry white wine,
such as Chardonnay

2-3tbsp veal stock

salt and freshly ground black pepper

First make the *pistou*, then cover and chill.

Break the stalks off the artichokes at their base, then cut off the pointed tips of the leaves and pull them gently away from the centre. Use a small spoon to scoop out any hairy choke. Brush the cut surfaces with lemon juice.

Heat the oil in a large sauté or frying pan. Add the onions and carrots and sweat them for 10 minutes until soft but not coloured.

Stir in the tomatoes and tomato purée, then add the artichokes in one layer, standing them upright on the bed of vegetables. Sprinkle in the garlic and basil and add the bouquet garni.

Add the wine and enough warm water to come half-way up the sides of the artichokes and bring to the simmer. Cover, lower the heat and cook for 1 ½ hours until the artichokes are tender, adding water if necessary.

Transfer the artichokes to a warmed plate. If the sauce is still liquid, boil until almost all the extra liquid has evaporated. Stir in the veal stock and the *pistou*, spoon on to a warmed platter and then arrange the artichokes on top.

TIAN DE COURGE A L'EPEAUTRE

Marrow and Einkorn Gratin

SERVES 4

450g/1lb marrow or summer squash, cut
into 2cm/¾ in cubes
3tbsp single cream
250g/8½ oz einkorn or pearl barley,
well rinsed
2 garlic cloves, peeled
25g/¾ oz Gruyère cheese, grated
1tbsp fresh parsley, finely chopped
100ml/3½ fl oz milk
2 eggs, lightly beaten
butter, for greasing dish
salt and freshly ground black pepper

FOR THE GARLIC BREAD

1 small baguette
1 garlic clove, halved
olive oil for drizzling

Make the garlic bread one day in advance.
Preheat the grill to medium. Slice the baguette
in two lengthways, rub with the cut sides of
the garlic clove, drizzle with olive oil and grill
until lightly browned.

On the day you want to make the dish,
preheat the oven to 150°C/300°F/gas mark 2.
Grease a *tian* or shallow gratin dish.

Remove the crust from the garlic bread and
cut into cubes. Put the marrow or squash,
cream and bread in a flameproof casserole
and season. Cover and put in the oven for
about 2 hours or until the marrow cooks and
reduces to a compote.

Meanwhile, put the einkorn or pearl barley
in a large saucepan and cover with twice its
volume of cold water. Place the saucepan over
a high heat and bring to the boil, uncovered,

then add the garlic cloves and a pinch of salt.
Cover tightly, lower the heat and simmer for
about 40 minutes or until the grains are
swollen. Turn off the heat and leave the pan
to stand, covered, for 10 minutes, then drain.

Remove the casserole from the oven and
increase the temperature to 190°C/375°F/gas
mark 5. Stir half the Gruyère cheese into the
casserole together with the parsley, milk, eggs
and einkorn or pearl barley. Spoon the
mixture into the prepared gratin dish, smooth
the surface and sprinkle the remaining
Gruyère cheese on top. Put the gratin dish in
the oven for 20 minutes or until the top
browns. Serve immediately.

PAVE DE SANDRE BRAISE AU BASILIC

Fillet of Zander in a Herb Crust with Fresh Basil

*Zander is a river fish with flaky white flesh and
a delicate flavour which sometimes needs a
boost. The herb crust begins life as a paste but,
during cooking, the butter melts into the fish.
(Illustrated opposite)*

SERVES 4

100g/3½ oz fresh white breadcrumbs
100g/3½ oz butter, softened
1 hard-boiled egg yolk
15g/½ oz button mushroom, finely chopped
25g/¾ oz shallot, finely chopped
1tsp fresh flat-leaf parsley, finely chopped
1tsp fresh chives, finely chopped
1tsp fresh basil, finely chopped
4 zander, perch or pike fillets, each
weighing 150g/5½ oz
200ml/7fl oz dry white wine or water
cayenne pepper
50g/1¾ oz butter, well chilled and diced
fresh basil leaves, roughly torn
salt and freshly ground black pepper

Preheat the oven to 220°C/425°F/gas mark 7.
Grease a gratin dish.

Put the breadcrumbs and butter into a bowl.
Then, with your finger, push the egg yolk
through a sieve into the bowl. Knead together.
Add the mushrooms, half the shallot, the
parsley, chives and basil and season. Knead a
second time until well blended.

Season the fish fillets and cover the skinless
side of each with some of the breadcrumb
mixture. Put the fillets in the gratin dish and
sprinkle the remaining shallot and the white
wine or equivalent quantiy of water around
the fillets. Season with a little cayenne pepper.
Put the gratin dish in the oven and cook for
about 10 minutes until a crust forms.

Remove the fish from the oven, transfer to a
serving platter and keep warm. Strain the
cooking liquid through a fine sieve into a
small saucepan. Bring the liquid to the boil
and cook until it is reduced and syrupy. Whisk
in the chilled butter, piece by piece, to make a
sauce. Put the sauce in a warmed sauce boat.

Strew fresh basil leaves over the fish and
serve with the sauce.

NOISETTES D'AGNEAU AUX TRUFFES

Truffled Lamb Noisettes

This is a refined version of a rustic recipe. If noisettes are unavailable, ask your butcher to make them up from a boned saddle of lamb. The quantity of truffles can be reduced.

SERVES 4

12 noisettes of lamb
55g/2oz black truffles, thinly sliced
1tbsp olive oil, plus extra
for brushing
4 tomatoes, peeled, seeded and
finely chopped
4 garlic cloves
4 sprigs of parsley
salt and freshly ground black pepper

Preheat the oven to 250°C/475°F/gas mark 9.

Remove the string from each noisette. Carefully separate the fat from the meat of each noisette and then put half the truffle slices between the fat and the flesh, reassemble and tie up with string. Put the lamb in a roasting tin, brush all over with olive oil and place in the oven for 10-15 minutes.

Meanwhile, heat 1 tablespoon of olive oil with 1 tablespoon of water in a small saucepan over a medium heat. Whisk the water and oil together, then add the remaining truffles and the tomatoes and cook, stirring occasionally, for 3-4 minutes. While the truffles and tomatoes are cooking, finely chop the garlic and parsley and mix together to make a *persillade*.

Remove the lamb from the oven and set aside. Add the *persillade* to the tomatoes and truffles, heat through and season to taste. Serve the noisettes with the tomato mixture.

DAUBE DE BOEUF

Beef Stew, Provençal Style

Daubes are stews cooked very slowly in a special earthenware pot called a daubière. *Traditionally, they would have been made with mutton or goat and stewed overnight. Today, most daubes are made from beef and they don't need cooking for so long. (Illustrated right)*

SERVES 4

1kg/2 ¼ lb chuck steak, cut into
cubes of 2cm/ ³⁄₄ in
100g/3 ½ oz pork belly, with its rind
25g/ ³⁄₄ oz lard
1 tbsp olive oil
1 large onion, chopped
2 carrots, cut into 5x1cm/2x ½ in batons
½ bottle red wine, such as Côtes de Provence
bouquet garni consisting of 1 sprig of
thyme, 1 bay leaf and a piece of celery stalk
sprig of parsley
piece of orange zest
6 black peppercorns, crushed
2 fresh or dried juniper berries, crushed
2 cloves
pinch of freshly grated nutmeg

Cut the rind off the belly of pork, then dice the meat and cut the rind into strips.

Melt the lard with the olive oil in a flame-proof casserole over a medium-high heat. Add the pork belly and rind and fry until they start to brown, then add the onion and carrots and cook until lightly browned.

Pour in the wine, add the chuck steak and the remaining ingredients. Add boiling water to cover, stir well and bring to the simmer. Lower the heat, cover and cook for 2-3 hours until the liquid is a glossy, dark sauce and the meat is tender. Taste and adjust seasoning.

CAILLES CONFITES AUX OLIVES

Casserole of Quail

This recipe was traditionally made with thrushes, although I have suggested using oven-ready quail which cuts the cooking time in half. Songbirds are, however, still shot all over the garrigues and hills of Provence. The law now prohibits their sale commercially but allows you to shoot them for your own pot. Dried juniper berries can be used instead of fresh if none are available.

SERVES 4

200g/7oz belly of pork, cut into
3x1cm/1 ½ x ½ in strips
200g/7oz black olives, stoned
8 oven-ready quail
4tbsp olive oil
4 garlic cloves, crushed
8 fresh juniper berries
2 sprigs of thyme
2 black peppercorns
2tbsp Cognac
salt and freshly ground black pepper

Preheat the oven to 180°C/350°F/Gas 4.

Put the pork strips and olives in a saucepan, cover with water and bring to a medium boil to blanch for 3 minutes. Drain, refresh under cold, running water and drain again. Pat dry with paper towels.

Season the quails, then put them in a large casserole. Scatter over the pork strips and olives and stir in the remaining ingredients. Cover the casserole tightly and cook for 45 minutes to 1 hour or until very tender.

Serve the birds with the cooking juices and accompany with a salad of bitter leaves or freshly cooked pasta.

LIEVRE EN DAUBE

Hare Stew

Rabbit and hare are still staple meats all over northern Provence and mostly shot wild. This daube is unusual in using white wine and lard, rather than red wine and olive oil.

SERVES 4

1 hare, skinned, cleaned and cut into 8 pieces
30g/1oz lard
200g/7oz pork belly, diced
1 onion, chopped
500ml/16fl oz light beef stock or water

FOR THE MARINADE

1 onion, quartered
2 garlic cloves, halved
bouquet garni consisting of 1 sprig of
thyme, 1 bay leaf and 1 sprig of parsley
½ bottle fruity white wine
1 tbsp sherry vinegar or red wine

One day in advance, place the hare in a non-metallic bowl. Add the onion, garlic, bouquet garni, wine and vinegar and leave the hare to marinate overnight in a cool place.

Melt the lard in a large flameproof casserole over a medium heat. Add the pork belly and chopped onion and cook, stirring frequently, until lightly browned.

Remove the hare pieces from the marinade and pat dry with paper towels. Add to the casserole and cook until lightly browned.

Place the stock in a saucepan and bring to the boil. Pour into the casserole along with the reserved marinade, including the onion, garlic and bouquet garni. Bring the liquid to the boil, cover and cook over a low heat for 1 hour until the hare is very tender. Remove the bouquet garni and serve in deep soup plates.

OREILLETTES

Little Pastry 'Ears'

These pastry strips are shaped to resemble ears when they puff up in the deep-fat fryer. Powdered with icing sugar, they used to be a New Year treat but patisseries now sell them all year round. They are not difficult to make at home but you must be sure to roll the dough almost to transparency and fry them very quickly in very hot oil for them to puff up and crisp properly.

SERVES 4
250g/8 ½ oz plain flour
pinch of salt
½ tsp baking powder
2 eggs, lightly beaten
55g/2oz butter, diced and softened
finely chopped zest of ½ lemon
1tsp orange flower water
1-1 ½ l/1 ¾ -2 ½ pt sunflower oil for deep-frying
45g/1 ½ oz icing sugar

Sift the flour, salt and baking powder into a large bowl. Make a well in the centre and add the eggs, butter, lemon zest and orange flower water. With your hands, mix together to form a dough, then knead the·dough in the bowl until it is smooth and silky. Cover the bowl with a cloth and leave the dough to rest in the refrigerator for about 2 hours.

Roll out the dough on a lightly-floured work surface. The thinner you roll it, the crunchier the *oreillettes* will be. Use a pastry wheel or knife to cut the dough into 10x4cm/4x1 ¾ in pieces. You should end up with 40-50 *oreillettes*. Make a diagonal slit in the centre of each, then fold one end of the *oreillette* through the slit so the pastry resembles an ear.

Heat the sunflower oil in a deep-fat fryer until it reaches a temperature of 195°C/385°F. Add the *oreillettes* a few at a time and fry for just a couple of seconds until they have puffed up and are golden brown in colour. Remove them from the pan with a slotted spoon as they cook and drain well on several layers of paper towels. Continue frying the rest of the *oreillettes* until all are done. Allow to cool and sift icing sugar over them before serving. Serve the *oreillettes* at room temperature, on their own or with coffee.

FOUGASSE

Flat Yeast Bread

Also called fouace *or* pompe, *this bread is always oval in shape and slashed with several holes like veins in a leaf. It represents Christ as the centrepiece of the* Treize Desserts *on Christmas Eve, when it is flavoured with orange flower water. It can also be studded with candied peel or made savoury with the addition of olives, anchovies, crispy bacon and without the sugar. (Illustrated opposite)*

MAKES 4 LOAVES
800g/1 ¾ lb white bread flour
1 tsp salt
25g/ ¾ oz caster sugar
1 sachet easy-blend dried yeast
2 eggs
5 tbsp olive oil
juice of 1 orange
1 tbsp orange flower water

Put the flour, salt, sugar and yeast in a large bowl and stir them together, then make a well in the centre.

Crack both the eggs into a measuring jug, then add the olive oil, orange juice and orange flower water and beat together thoroughly. Add enough hot water to make the mixture up to 450ml/15fl oz.

Pour the liquids into the bowl containing the dry ingredients and mix together with your hands to form a soft dough. Turn out on to a lightly floured surface and knead for about 10 minutes until the dough is smooth and light. Return the dough to the bowl, cover with a damp cloth and leave in a warm place for about 45 minutes until doubled in size.

Knock back the dough, then turn it out and quickly knead again on a lightly floured surface. Divide the dough into 4 pieces and roll out each one into a 20x15cm/8x6in oval, about 1cm/ ½ in thick. Cut 5-6 slits in each loaf to resemble the veins on a leaf, then pull the slits apart so they won't close up when the loaves are baked. Place the loaves on a lightly oiled baking tray, cover with a damp cloth and leave to rise again in a warm place for about 45 minutes.

Meanwhile, preheat the oven to 200°C/400°F/gas mark 6. Bake the loaves for 20-25 minutes until they are golden and sound hollow if tapped on the underside. Leave to cool on a wire rack.

*RIGHT BELOW The higgledy-piggledy tumble
of houses in the old port of Villefranche-sur-Mer
reflects the world of colour and sunlight
which abounds in the coastal villages
of Alpes Maritimes. Despite occupying acres of
prime Côte d'Azur, the port remains
unspoilt. Although the Maritimes
area is a land of sun and sea, the larger Alpes
area has a considerably harsher
landscape and way of life.*

*ABOVE The sparkling array of fish found daily in
the markets of Alpes Maritimes reflects
gold, silver and copper lustres.*
*TOP ROW, LEFT Brightly-coloured citrus fruits
undergo the long process of crystallization at the
Confiserie des Gorges du Loup (see page 115).*
*TOP ROW, CENTRE AND RIGHT A sober, Victorian
influence, perhaps, produced the architecture
in Grasse which looks more at home in
England than in the South of France. But there's
no mistaking Provençal tradition in these
old boules, on sale in Nice market.*

ALPES MARITIMES

The Côte d'Azur; the French Riviera. The words still have the power to conjure up glamour, although in truth, there is little glamorous about this coastline of the Alpes Maritimes in high summer when most tourists go. Then, beaches are overcrowded and prices are sky high as the canny Provençaux try to pocket enough cash to tide them over the out-of-season months. Better, by far, to go there between autumn and spring, as the first British and American tourists did, when the locals are noticeably more friendly and the former fishing ports regain something of their gentility and original charm.

Few visitors, however, explore the Alpes Maritimes themselves: the range of mountains scored by deep gorges and narrow valleys that rise dramatically behind the *corniches*, or coastal roads, which run between La Napoule and Menton on the Italian border. Here also are some of the most inaccessible hilltop villages, such as Peillon and Peille, as well as some of the most fashionable, like Mougins and Vence.

Effectively cut off by these mountains from the rest of France before the coming of the railway, Nice and its hinterland did not actually become part of France until 1860. Before then, it was part of the Italian kingdom of Savoy. Indeed, the area around Saorge and Tende, in the far north-east of the Alpes Maritimes, did not join France officially until 1947. So the Italian influence is still strong, especially in the food – a combination of Mediterranean French and Piedmontese Italian. Up in the poor Alpine villages along the Italian border there is a strong and continuing tradition of pasta and gnocchi, adopted here because of their cheap but filling qualities. They are never served as a separate course as in Italy, but to accompany a *tian* or daube. Down on the richer and more sophisticated coast, *soupe au pistou*, *ratatouille* and *salade niçoise* are culinary reminders that this part of Provence is as Italian as it is French.

The prosperity of this *département* is relatively recent. Before access to the markets of northern France, the economy depended on fishing and peasant farming, which in turn, depended on the weather. Olives and citrus crops could be wiped out by a severe frost; in fact, it was the failure of an orange harvest that led to the building of the famous Promenade des Anglais in Nice in the 1820s. It was a make-work project, paid for by the resident English colony to tide the farmers through a disastrous year.

Olives and citrus fruit are still important crops – and still as vulnerable to frost – but equally important are the mini mountain ranges of greenhouses which protect delicate vegetables, all to be sold at premium prices, mainly to restaurants and hotels. Only about twelve kilometres north of Nice, acres of glass clad the west bank of the river Var near Carros, housing the fresh herbs, courgette flowers, tomatoes and salad leaves. These include the mixed sowings of greens and herbs known as *mesclun* that market gardeners such as the Auda family dedicate themselves to growing year round. After all, who needs seasons here? Still of major importance are the crops of jasmine, rose and orange flowers, grown on the hillsides around Grasse for the perfume industry. Rose and orange flower water are also used as flavourings in cooking.

CREATIVE CUISINE

This is the only part of Provence to have any tradition of *haute cuisine*, or where restaurants have played an important role in changing culinary habits. When wealthy English and Americans flocked here to enjoy the mild winters in the second half of the nineteenth century, they built villas along the coast from Cannes to Menton. Soon, some of the most exclusive restaurants in Europe were opened and the coastline and its littoral is still the most sophisticated part of Provence. But the underlying simplicity of Provençal cuisine once more shines through in the dishes and the philosophies of the famous chefs who live and work here today: the '*cuisine du soleil*' of Roger Vergé, the elder statesman of modern Provençal cooking at Mougins (see page 119); the refined fish cookery of Serge Philippin, chef of the Restaurant de Bacon on Cap d'Antibes (see page 118); the creative balancing acts with traditional yet subtle combinations of olive oil, garlic and herbs, performed in Cannes by Christian Willer at La Palme d'Or in the Martinez Hotel and by Jacques Chibois at Le Royal Gray in the Gray d'Albion Hotel. Both, interestingly are 'incomers': Christian Willer from Alsace and Jacques Chibois from Bordeaux.

The best way to discover the culinary traditions of this part of Provence is to take a leisurely stroll round the *vieille ville* of Nice. The old town has retained its pre-Riviera charm: narrow, twisting, dark streets leading up to a hilltop citadel and down to the Cours Saleya bordering the sea. Filled with stalls, all piled with a cornucopia of the freshest fruit and vegetables and lined with cafés, bars and restaurants, it is a vivid reminder of the town's pre-resort history, dating back to its Greek foundation in the fourth century B.C.

The maze of old streets is worth exploring for its sumptuous architecture – baroque churches and a neoclassical opera house – but is also crammed with tiny shops selling equally sumptuous food. Here are Alziari, makers of the favourite olive oil of long-time mayor of Nice, Jacques Médecin; Henri Auer, famous for chocolates and crystallized fruit; Charcuterie Saint-François for the best charcuterie in town; fresh pasta and ravioli in infinite variety; the Four au Bois where André Espuno bakes more than thirty kinds of bread, and La Mérenda, Jean Giusti's tiny restaurant where you sit on stools watching the chef work miracles, producing his famous *pasta au pistou*, daubes, deep-fried courgette flowers and other specialities from a kitchen the size of a postage stamp. Get there early and don't try to book: La Mérenda has never seen the need for a telephone.

Pasta, polenta, *pistou* (Genoese pesto), *pissaladière*: the culinary influence of Italy is strong. But the Niçois have also adopted some surprising dishes from their foreign visitors.

*OPPOSITE 'New' and 'old' Nice are neatly divided
by a wide esplanade running north
from the jardin Albert Premier to the place
Garibaldi. To its east, the streets of the
old town (top) include some of the best bakeries
(centre). The Cours Saleya is the scene
of a variety of fish restaurants (bottom).
ABOVE Numerous cafés offer tranquil refuge.
LEFT Tempting dishes such as this paella are sold
as street food all over Nice.*

STREET FOOD

*All along the Riviera, and, increasingly
inland, you will find stalls and vans selling a
variety of street food. Socca, a thick
pancake made with a batter of chickpea flour,
olive oil and water and cooked quickly on large,
flat pans, is native to Nice and the traditional
mid-morning snack, or mérenda, of
building workers. Today it is still hawked on
barrows topped with charcoal stoves but is more
likely to be seen around the Cours Saleya
market square in the old town, vying for custom
with vans selling pissaladière, another
Niçois snack (see pages 122-3).
My favourite, though, is pan bagnat, the best and
the messiest of sandwiches. Originally,
pan bagnat consisted of pieces of stale bread
added to a salade niçoise and left to
soak up the oil and tomato juice. The modern
version reverses the procedure: a
special small round loaf is cut horizontally in
two and some of the bread scooped out of the
centre. The inside is then rubbed with
garlic, sprinkled generously with olive oil,
seasoned and filled with salade niçoise. The two
halves are pressed firmly together, wrapped
tightly in aluminium foil and chilled
until the bread is moist through.*

Jacques Médecin, before his fall from power amid charges of scandal and corruption made by, among others, Graham Greene in his pamphlet *J'Accuse*, wrote *Cuisine Niçoise*, a rather charming cookery book in which he recalls his grandmother, when he was a small boy, making what she called 'ploum-pudding' for Christmas and New Year. For years he assumed it was a local speciality.

In return, Nice has given its name to a surprising array of dishes, from *salade niçoise* to *tripes à la niçoise*, with almost anything cooked with tomatoes and garlic, in between. It has also developed an odd speciality of its own: *estocaficada*. This is a liquid stew of dried (not salted) cod, tomatoes, olives, garlic and potatoes with a powerfully off-putting smell. Those who can defy the warnings of their nose will find it relatively mild although it is something of an acquired taste. This symbol of true Niçois gastronomy is not, perhaps, to be tried at home. Dried cod takes much longer to reconstitute than salt cod, and

M. Médecin's recipe instructs you to saw it into sections and leave under a dripping cold water tap for eight days. There are rumours that a slightly faster, but less savoury, method is to suspend the fish in a lavatory cistern which achieves the necessary frequent changes of water every time it is flushed!

More universally popular and much easier to prepare, is *mesclun*, the salad of mixed leaves and herbs which Nice also claims as its own and which is now *de rigueur* in fashionable restaurants everywhere. No one is sure of its origins, although at the turn of the century *mesclun* grown by Franciscan fathers in Cimiez (now a suburb of Nice) was thought special enough to be given as a gift. Equally, no one can agree on the authentic mix of leaves although the aim should be to combine mild and bitter tastes and soft and crunchy textures. Typically, leaf lettuces such as oak leaf and cos will be tossed with peppery rocket and dandelion leaves, chervil and curly endive. The critical thing is to pick the ingredients young – reflecting the origin of *mesclun* as a way of using up vegetable thinnings.

ABOVE AND OPPOSITE TOP Modern Cannes
was founded by Lord Brougham in 1834 when a
cholera outbreak in Italy forced him to retreat
here. Within a decade, Cannes was the favourite
resort of European aristocracy. Today, the
palm trees and sun loungers that fringe its
private beaches typify Cannes to most visitors.
OPPOSITE CENTRE AND BELOW Old Cannes
centres on Le Suquet, and still thrives in the
streets around the Forville market with
food shops selling everything from fresh pasta to
the kind of prepared food that means you
need never cook again.

But this coastline's culinary roots have always been cosmopolitan, going back to the Phocean traders, who settled in Nice and Antiopolis, now Antibes, in the sixth century B.C. As elsewhere in Provence, they came for olive oil. The oil of this region is different again in texture and taste from that of Nyons or Maussane, with olives picked black and ripe from January to March. A specific variety grows here, and only here: the Cailletier, also known as the *olive de Nice*, is small, wrinkled and black and cured in a herbed brine. Many people still cure their own olives every winter and, while they are ubiquitous as a Niçois pre-meal nibble to accompany an aperitif, and essential to a proper *salade niçoise*, they are rarely seen outside Provence.

These olives are also made into oil at mills such as the Moulin de la Brague at Opio, near Grasse. Olives have been pressed here since at least 1426 (the furthest the records go back) and now by Roger, the seventh generation of the Michel family to own the Moulin. Local people bring their own small crops of olives here every year, keeping enough oil for their own use and selling the rest to the Moulin for a little extra income – if their crop is accepted (most mills will only press quantities of one hundred and forty kilos and upwards). Quality is controlled and, as a notice at the mill reads, 'all dubious olives will be sent back'. Too green, and they impart a bitterness to the oil; too ripe and they produce too much acidity. Olives, says M. Michel, turn black from the outside in and are perfect for oil just before the colour reaches the stone. So oil is made here between November and March, depending on the ripeness of the fruit. With some regret, and to complaints from his older clients, Roger Michel now filters his yellow-green oil. Today, most customers demand a clear product that does not contain any residue.

Few fishermen can make a living along this stretch of Provence's coast: the old ports are now tourist resorts and much of the water is now polluted. *Poissonneries* may have glistening displays of John Dory, sea bass, monkfish, mullet, bream, snapper, *rascasse*, sardines, piles of tiny rockfish and shellfish of all kinds, but most have been packed in ice and 'imported' from Marseille or the Atlantic coast. It is at markets like the ones in Antibes or Forville in Cannes that you see the relative poverty, in quantity, of the local catch. Here, sometimes only half a dozen fishwives can offer a sparse selection of *rouget*, *rascasse*, mullet and John Dory. But they sell quickly and at a high price, for these are ultra-fresh, prized for their quality. They have never 'slept on ice'.

Cannes is one of the few former fishing villages turned into resorts that still manages to retain some of its own identity even at the height of summer or during the Film Festival. The port is guarded by a steep hill, Le Suquet, and flanked by the old quarter of narrow streets with shops filled with mouthwatering fresh pasta, breads, pastries and cheeses from all over France. The rue Meynardier, in particular, is a focus for a wide variety of sumptuous food shops. Alongside the harbour stands the Palais des Festivals, a recently-built and very ugly full-stop before the wide sweep of promenade along the boulevard de la Croisette. Fronted by golden beaches kept scrupulously clean (many of them are private beaches), the boulevard is lined with such *grande dame* hotels as the Carlton and the Martinez, together with serried terraces of apartments which seem to house many more blue-rinsed ladies and small dogs than glamorous blonde starlets.

LEFT AND FAR LEFT Like so many of the Riviera's towns, popularized and developed by nineteenth-century European aristocracy, Grasse has kept its old town separate and virtually unspoilt. Teetering perilously on steep terraces cut into the slopes of a hillside behind Cannes, it commands sweeping views of the Golfe de Napoule almost twenty kilometres away. BELOW The tranquility of Grasse extends to the Place aux Aires on market days where, for once, flowers play as important a part as food; not surprising, perhaps, since Grasse is the perfume capital of France.

ABOVE Grasse's most famous son is Jean-Honoré Fragonard, the eighteenth-century painter whose great canvases, The Pursuit of Love, hang in New York's Frick Collection.

BACK TO THE PAST

Once the tourists have gone back home, the Riviera seems to breathe a sigh of relief and revert to the way of life of half a century ago. The men, whose lined, weather-beaten faces as well as their dark stockiness seem to be passed down through each generation, can at last play *pétanque* (the Provençal version of *boules*) in peace. Shopkeepers and market stallholders become noticeably more friendly and restaurant prices approach something like sanity. Now the massed racks of T-shirts, sunhats, espadrilles and tacky souvenirs recede from the narrow streets of old Nice, Antibes and Cannes and the charcuteries, patisseries, *traiteurs*, boulangeries and fromageries can be seen, their mouthwatering window displays once again magnets for passers-by. For, while the local economy may depend on the annual influx of the tourist dollar, the mark and the yen, the local people have never been known to neglect their stomachs.

As you go north into the Haut-Pays and the Alps proper, you become aware of a more robust and rustic cooking, one which Patrick Boscq avidly promotes at his modest restaurant, Maître Boscq, in Grasse's old town. Here, he cooks *Caillettes*, a terrine of chopped pork and its liver marbled with chard leaves (see page 123); escargots in basil butter and, his great speciality, *Lou Fassum*, or stuffed cabbage, a recipe that dates as far back as Roman times (see page 127). The recipe he gave me was, he stressed, the modern version: it does contain some meat.

In the past, meat was as scarce in these hills as in the other mountain ranges and high plateaux of Provence. Today, animal husbandry and cheese making are rarities, both meat and cheese being easy to import. Hunting continues but the mountain slopes are so steep that this, too, seems to be a dying tradition. Many of the houses in the remote *villages perchés* have been bought up and turned into weekend homes and, just as the inhabitants on the Côte d'Azur rely on summer tourists for income, so those in the mountains rely on winter tourists flocking to the modern ski resorts such as the dramatically-named Isola 2,000 which is less than one hundred kilometres from Nice, and where skiers are virtually guaranteed snow and sun.

Alpes Maritimes is not vineyard country. However, there is Bellet, a tiny *appellation* (there are only four *domaines*) high on the hillsides of the Var and still within the commune of Nice, which, therefore, can claim to be the only French city with an *appellation contrôlée* vineyard within its boundaries. After years of gentle decline, the vineyards have been revived in recent years and the wine 'relaunched' by the Bagnis family, owners of Château Crémat, the main producer. Grown on just seventy hectares of stony soil around the walled village of Saint-Roman-de-Bellet, the vines benefit from their height and a cool microclimate: sea breezes blow up the valley by day and cold Alpine air blows down by night. This cooler climate gives the wine a finesse and sophistication which is rare for Provence. The reds can keep for a few years, the rosés are smooth yet firm, but the whites can be outstanding: pale and straw-coloured with a bouquet of wildflowers and the weight of a white Burgundy. Only forty thousand bottles of the white wine are made each year, so it is expensive and rarely seen far from home.

TOP AND ABOVE At their mill near Opio, the Michel family sometimes flavours the olive oil with various herbs and spices. These oils are for sale in the shop adjoining the mill.

THE GREATEST CHEF OF ALL

Auguste Escoffier's home was in the small village of Villeneuve-Loubet near Nice. The man whose name is still synonymous with French classic cuisine was born, the son of a blacksmith, in 1846 and apprenticed to his restaurateur uncle in Nice in 1859, the year before the town was ceded from Italy to France. At the age of nineteen, he moved to Paris to work at Le Petit Moulin Rouge, a restaurant where the private rooms were occasionally patronized by the future King Edward VII. In 1876, he returned to Provence, opening his own restaurant, Le Faisan Doré in Cannes. There he met César Ritz and they began their long collaboration, creating the reputations of London's Savoy and Carlton hotels over thirty years around the turn of the century.

The man who invented Pêche Melba (a combination of vanilla ice cream, poached peaches and raspberry sauce), for diva Nelly Melba in 1892, also introduced frogs' legs to England, serving them with a paprika sauce and listing them on the menu as 'Nymphes à la Rose'. Diners raved about them, without realizing exactly what they were. In a similar vein, he always beat eggs with a knife speared with a clove of garlic. Right to the end of her life, Sarah Bernhardt claimed a hatred of garlic while considering Escoffier's scrambled eggs to be the best she ever ate.

His house has now been made into a museum exhibiting pans and kitchen utensils of the period, including a mechanical device he invented for stoning fruit and olives and an unlikely-looking contraption claimed to be the earliest forerunner of the food processor. There is a curiously modern-looking 'traditional' Provençal kitchen and, upstairs, a room crammed with thousands of menus of not-so-dainty dishes laid before kings and presidents and, for no apparent reason, a typewritten list of all the kings and queens of England from Ecgberht in A.D. 827 up to the present day.

But, until he died (at the age of eighty-nine in 1935), Escoffier never forgot his Provençal roots and, while the menus collected here seem extravagantly rich and lengthy to us, they were, in fact, relatively short and simple. For all his decorative flourishes, Escoffier developed his cooking according to the principles of nutrition and digestion and was the first of the great chefs to base his sauces on a light veal stock rather than on the more common flour-based roux.

Not far away is Biot, an almost too-pretty and thus too-touristy village and, just outside, the Verrerie de Biot which makes the famous, and expensive, bubbled glassware. You can still watch the glassblowers at work and ponder over how they get the bubbles into the glass (easy: just add a pinch of carbon-dioxide-producing salt). This once-small enterprise has grown to almost theme-park dimensions over the last forty years, with bars, cafés and, of course, shops, selling not only the glassware but also glazed earthenware and linen, patterned to match. You either love or hate this stuff. I think the glassware suits its home climate but tends to look rather twee once it has been transported to colder, northern lights. There is also a gallery showing a wonderful collection of the modern glass designs of Biot-trained artist Jean-Claude Novaro and another constantly-changing exhibition representing young designers from all over the world.

ABOVE Auguste Escoffier is justly celebrated in his home town of Villeneuve-Loubet even though he spent much of his time converting the 'heathen' in London hotels, notably the Savoy and the Carlton. His birthplace is now a museum, celebrating a working life of over sixty years. An inventive chef, he also had a practical side, perfecting a fruit/olive stoner and encouraging the preservation of fruit and vegetables by canning. Shortly before he left the Carlton in 1919, the hotel was damaged by fire. Escoffier emerged to announce to the gawping crowd: 'the thousands of chickens I have roasted here did not succeed in taking their revenge'. He retired to Monte Carlo where he had worked for several seasons in the 1880s.

CRYSTALLIZED FRUIT PRODUCER

Fruits confits, or crystallized fruits, have a long, delicious tradition in Provence. One of the oldest ways and, before the days of canning and refrigeration, the only way to keep soft fruit through the winter months, crystallizing fruits now makes them a very sweet and expensive luxury. But a shop window full of their gleam and colour is barely resistable, and no one even tries to resist at Christmas when they are a popular gift, laid out like jewels in wooden boxes or baskets. Indeed, a large proportion of the crystallized fruit trade occurs during the Christmas rush. The traditional centre was Apt in the Vaucluse, but most production there is now industrial. Specialized producers still exist, however, scattered around the region in places such as Sault in Vaucluse and Saint-Rémy-de-Provence in Bouches-du-Rhône. One of the most attractive is the Confiserie des Gorges du Loup, at Pont-du-Loup, high in the hills behind Grasse.

Fruits with flavours strong enough still to be tasted through a stong impregnation of sugar fare best. At the confiserie, clementines, cherries, apricots, greegages, whole melons and pineapples, each type of fruit kept separate, are first pricked to allow the sugar to enter, then blanched for several hours. They are then slowly boiled for a few hours each day in deep-sided, unlined copper bowls in increasingly strong, steam-prepared sugar syrup. The soaking-in-syrup process takes the humidity out of the fruit and feeds it sugar. The fruits are then cooled, still steeped in the syrup, in conical terracotta dishes. These repeated boilings and coolings, and daily additions of more sugar, go on for forty to sixty days, depending on the size of the fruit, until they are fully saturated with syrup. This lengthy process explains their high cost and it cannot be speeded up without the fruit losing its shape. Once fully saturated, however, the fruit will keep indefinitely if covered in its syrup, to be drained and either dusted with sugar or dipped in boiling syrup for a glacé finish, just before sale.

Aside from crystallized fruit, the confiserie also makes a wide selection of citrus fruit jams which have a much sweeter taste than marmalade. Another unusual gift, hand-made in small quantities at the Confiserie des Gorges du Loup, is a delicate pink preserve made out of rose petals. This preserve is highly-scented with a distinctive flavour, and is something of an acquired taste.

TOP *Small but perfectly formed, clementines are a speciality grown on the Alpes Maritimes hillsides between Nice and the Italian border. At the Confiserie des Gorges du Loup they are crystallized in sugar syrup but can also be saturated in alcohol.*
ABOVE *Orange and lemon peel is also candied before being either rolled in sugar or dipped in bitter chocolate.*
LEFT AND FAR LEFT *The Confiserie also makes a range of quality jams from citrus fruits and a highly-scented pink preserve from rose petals.*

ORANGE FLOWER WATER

*The blossoms that scent the hills for
miles around Grasse every spring are mostly
harvested for use in the perfume industry.
But two, orange and rose, have culinary uses.
Orange flower water is used to give a
more elusive aroma than would zest or juice,
to a variety of cakes, custards and
breads – most famously the Christmas
fougasse. This essential oil, properly called
néroli, also has medicinal properties: one
to three drops on a sugar lump taken several
times a day, is supposed to halt heart
palpitations and cure chronic diarrhoea.
Rose water is distilled from the petals of the
damask rose which grew wild in France and,
even though it has more Middle Eastern
associations (Turkish Delight, for example) it is
also used to scent creams, custards,
blancmanges, and, sometimes, nougat. These
'waters' are actually distillates, made
in the same way as cognac or whisky and, drop
for drop, about as expensive. This is not
surprising when you're told that it takes one
ton of blossoms to make six hundred
litres of distillate. For those who find it
impossible to visualize a ton of flower petals,
that computes at about two kilograms or four
pounds weight of petals per litre.*

But, of course, this region is also famous for the twentieth-century painters who lived here, especially Picasso, Matisse, Chagall, Léger and Cocteau. They moved into the little hill towns, like Le Cannet, Mougins, Vence, Vallauris and Saint-Paul-de-Vence, and brought a respectable (by comparison) touch of the Bohemian to the louche lives of those denizens of the Riviera who openly courted scandal, such as Isadora Duncan, Somerset Maugham, Scott Fitzgerald, Ernest Hemingway and Frank Harris, he of the self-proclaimed legendary sexual exploits.

A great deal of the painters' and sculptors' art can easily be seen today, primarily at the great indoor and outdoor galleries of the Fondation Maeght near Saint-Paul-de-Vence and in museums devoted to individual artists: Picasso at Antibes, Léger at Biot, Cocteau at Menton, and Matisse and Chagall at Cimiez near Nice. There is also a restaurant/hotel hung with their art, the Colombe d'Or in Saint-Paul-de-Vence. It was opened in the 1920s by Paul Roux, a former farmer, who followed the nineteenth-century French tradition of accepting paintings and sculpture instead of money and then started collecting for himself. The collection is open to the public, but the entrance fee – the price of a meal – is costly!

Some of these great artists left living legacies as gifts. The great Matisse Chapelle de Rosaire at Vence is striking with its eloquently simple black line drawings against a background of white tiles; Cocteau's aquatic Chapelle de Saint-Pierre in Villefranche is dedicated to the local fishermen and his allegorical paintings decorate the wedding room of Menton's town hall; Picasso's Guernica-like La Guerre et la Paix (War and Peace) covers the walls of the twelfth-century vaults of a chapel in Vallauris, and was given to him to paint exactly as he wished, as a seventieth birthday present from the grateful potters of the town.

Picasso had earned the gratitude of the potters of Vallauris with his ceramic designs for the local Atelier Madoura workshop and pottery when he moved to the town in the late 1940s. Inspired by the sculpture of Suzanne Ramié, whose family owned Madoura, he designed a range of plates and bowls which the workshops still make and sell. Vallauris had had a reputation for its pottery since Roman times, but it had almost died out as an industry. Picasso singlehandedly revived the craft and Vallauris has traded on the connection ever since. Some potteries still make the traditional gracefully-curved earthenware pots used for storing olive oil since Roman times. Sadly, though, the town is now wall-to-wall with more than a hundred pottery shops awash with the sort of cheap souvenirs that give real meaning to the word vulgarity. Picasso may have played a major part in reviving the ceramics industry but, unfortunately, he couldn't control its taste.

Even if you are not an admirer of Picasso, the Madoura Gallery itself is an oasis. So, for a different reason, is the Nérolium Co-operative, run for the local market gardeners and stocked mostly with seeds, fertilizers and garden tools. They also sell their members' honeys, jams and their own orange flower and rose water, distilled each May and not really expensive when you consider that it takes one ton of blossoms to make six hundred litres of liquid. Similarly, orange flowers and roses are distilled for cosmetic or culinary use in the distilleries aroud Vallauris (see page 115). The Christmas *fougasse* (or *fouace* in Provençal dialect), essential component of the *Treize Desserts* on Christmas Eve (see page 92), is flavoured with orange flower water.

OPPOSITE BELOW The great names of Impressionism make their presence felt all over the French Riviera, sometimes expressed in small enclaves such as this charming mosaic-floored amphitheatre of the Théâtre Cocteau on Cap d'Ail near Monaco. Jean Cocteau also decorated the Chapelle de Saint-Pierre at Villefranche-sur-Mer and the municipal wedding room in Menton's town hall. Pierre Bonnard painted many rose-tinted views of the house at Le Bosquet close to Cannes, where he lived for his last twenty years.
OPPOSITE ABOVE No one made a bigger impression than Pablo Picasso who lived and worked in several parts of Provence from the 1940s until his death in 1973. Curiously little written about, the Musée Picasso looks out across the bay from the centre of Antibes' old town. Also known by its historic name, Château Grimaldi, this small castle was given to Picasso by the mayor of Antibes in 1946 to use as a studio. He spent six months there and, a few years later, donated a large number of works (tapestries and ceramics as well as paintings, drawings and sculptures). The museum also contains work by other contemporary artists, including these two sculptures by Germaine Richter.

RESTAURANT DE BACON

BOULEVARD BACON, 06600 CAP D'ANTIBES, TEL 93 61 50 02

The Restaurant de Bacon, on Cap d'Antibes, is a cool, white, glass-wrapped room with stunning views across the blue, sparkling waters of the bay of Antibes towards the old port. It gives the impression of dining on board a luxurious ocean liner. The restaurant is owned by the Sordello family and the kitchen has been run by chef Serge Philippin for the last decade. Under his rule, it has become justly famed for its bouillabaisse, *acclaimed, and generally accepted, as the best to be found anywhere along the coast of Provence. If you are to eat just one* bouillabaisse *while you are in Provence, this is the place to do it.*

BOUILLABAISSE

Provençal Fish Stew

Serge Philippin is of the tomatoes and potatoes bouillabaisse *school and he cooks the whole fish in its own stock, adding it to the broth just* before serving, which explains its clarity of flavour. If you can't find one of the fish listed in the recipe, it can be replaced by another. For example, turbot will perfectly replace John Dory. M. Philippin's recipe for rouille *is a more refined version of the traditional Provençal recipe (see page 34).*

(see page 34)

SERVES 4

FOR THE BROTH

150ml/5fl oz olive oil
2 small onions, thinly sliced
whites of 2 small leeks, thinly sliced
2 garlic heads, halved crosswise
½ celery stalk, thinly sliced
15g/ ½ oz tomato purée
1 tomato, peeled, seeded and chopped
2kg/4 ½ lb rockfish, cleaned
1tsp fresh thyme, finely chopped
2 bay leaves
1tbsp fennel seeds
1 fresh, whole chilli pepper
1tsp fresh tarragon leaves, finely chopped
pinch of saffron
4 potato slices, each cut the size of a finger
salt and freshly ground black pepper
16 slices of baguette, toasted

FOR COOKING THE FISH

850ml/1 ½ pt fish stock
1.5kg/3 ½ lb John Dory, scaled and cleaned
350g/12oz *rascasse rouge* (scorpion fish), scaled and cleaned
400g/14oz weever fish, scaled and cleaned
400g/14oz gurnard, scaled and cleaned
350g/12oz monkfish, skinned and cut into 4 thick slices

FOR THE ROUILLE

2 egg yolks
250ml/8fl oz groundnut oil
4 garlic cloves, crushed
pinch of cayenne pepper
pinch of crushed saffron strands
pinch of salt

Begin by making the broth. Put the olive oil in a very large stockpot over a medium heat. Lower the heat, add the onions, leeks, garlic and celery, then cover and cook for about

7 minutes until all the vegetables are soft but not coloured.

Add the tomato purée and cook for another 4 minutes, stirring constantly. Stir in the tomatoes, rockfish, thyme, bay leaves, fennel, chilli peppers and tarragon. Add 2l/3½ pt water and 1 tablespoon of salt and rapidly bring to the boil, then boil for 10 minutes.

Meanwhile, make the *rouille*. Put the egg yolks in a food processor and blend together. With the motor running, add the oil in a steady stream to make a mayonnaise. Add the garlic, cayenne, saffron and salt to taste and process briefly to blend. Transfer to a serving bowl, cover and chill.

Take the stockpot off the heat and stir the ingredients together. Pass everything in batches through a food processor or a mouli-légumes fitted with its largest blade, then again with a smaller blade. Strain the purée through a sieve lined with a piece of muslin, pressing hard to extract all the juices and finally wringing the cloth.

Stir in the saffron and seasoning. Put the potato 'fingers' into a saucepan and add a ladle or two of the broth and enough water to cover, then bring to the boil and cook for 10 minutes or until tender. Drain, transfer to a serving dish and keep warm.

Put the fish stock in the rinsed-out stockpot and bring to the boil. Add the fish individually, starting with the largest. Allow 10 minutes cooking time for the John Dory, 5 minutes for the *rascasse rouge*, weever fish and gurnard, and about 2 minutes for the monkfish slices. Carefully remove the fish and arrange on a serving platter. Taste and season the broth, pour into a large tureen and keep warm.

Present the fish and fillet them at the table. Distribute between 4 deep soup plates. Add a potato to each and ladle over the hot broth. Serve with the *rouille* and croutons.

LE RELAIS A MOUGINS

PLACE DE LA MAIRIE, 06250 MOUGINS, TEL 93 90 03 47

André Surmain created one of the first truly great restaurants in the United States — Lutèce in Manhattan — more than thirty years ago. In 1973 he sold it to his chef, André Soltner, moved to Majorca and opened a restaurant there. A Spanish lady had come into his life and, as André says 'I've always followed the women in my life.' A few years later, the woman in his life was French and, by 1977, he found himself in Mougins, a hilltop village behind Cannes. Of course he opened a restaurant: Le Relais à Mougins, in the village square. Surmain and his chef, Philippe Daguier, concentrate on robust dishes inspired by traditional recipes of the region. Surmain emphasizes that today his food must be 'good and tasty. Back to basics really.'

SABAYON DE FRUITS ROUGES AU MARSALA

Red Fruit Zabaglione
(*Illustrated right*)

SERVES 8
4 egg yolks
1tbsp caster sugar
1tbsp Marsala
200g/7oz strawberries
150g/5½oz raspberries or other red fruit
100g/3½oz wild strawberries
1tbsp icing sugar

Preheat the oven to 110°C/230°F/gas mark ¼.

Put the egg yolks, caster sugar and Marsala in a small non-aluminium saucepan over a low heat. Stir constantly until the sugar melts and the mixture thickens. Now begin whisking vigorously, gradually increasing the heat until the mixture is lukewarm. Remove from the heat and whisk to a light froth.

Preheat the grill to high. Arrange the fruit in 8 flameproof serving bowls and put in the oven for 3-4 minutes to barely warm the fruit.

Spoon the frothy mixture over the fruits and dust lightly with icing sugar. Grill in batches for 2-3 minutes each, to lightly colour the tops.

SOUPE AU PISTOU

Spring Vegetable Soup with Basil and Garlic Sauce

This is a spring-time soup in Provence made with fresh, shelled haricot beans. Most of us will have to substitute dried or tinned beans for the fresh haricot beans. If you can only find large broad beans, blanch them first and then slip them out of their outer skins before cooking. You can vary the other vegetables, but they should be young. The pistou is essential and should be added immediately before serving. (Illustrated opposite, front)

SERVES 4
**pistou (see right)
125g/4 ½ oz fresh haricot beans, shelled
(or 55g/2oz tinned haricot beans, drained and rinsed)
75g/2 ½ oz tomatoes, peeled, seeded and roughly chopped
55g/2oz potatoes, peeled and cut into 1cm/ ½ in dice
55g/2oz carrots, cut into 1cm/ ½ in dice
1 stalk celery, cut into 1cm/ ½ in dice
75g/2 ½ oz French beans, topped and tailed and cut into 1cm/ ½ in lengths
55g/2oz fresh baby broad beans, shelled
55g/2oz courgettes, unpeeled and cut into 1cm/ ½ in dice
55g/2oz vermicelli, broken into pieces
salt and freshly ground black pepper**

Make the *pistou*, cover and chill. Bring 2l/3 ½ pints of water to the boil in a large saucepan over a high heat. Add the haricot beans, tomatoes, potatoes, carrots and celery to the water, season and bring to the simmer, then cover the pan and cook over a low heat for 45 minutes, stirring occasionally.

Stir in the French beans, broad beans and courgettes and continue simmering for 15 minutes. Add the vermicelli and cook for 5-6 minutes until the pasta is just *al dente*.

Stir a few spoonfuls of the broth into the *pistou*, then either add all the *pistou* to the soup and stir together well just before serving, or serve the *pistou* separately so people can add as much or as little as they wish.

PISTOU

Basil and Garlic Sauce

Pistou *means 'pounded' in the* Niçois *dialect (from the Italian,* pestare*) and resembles the Genoese pesto sauce, but without the pine nuts. It can be made in large batches and kept for several weeks in the fridge, packed tightly into jars and covered with a layer of olive oil. Use tossed with freshly cooked pasta or added to soups, as above. When using it hot, heat very gently. Do not let it cook or it will become bitter.*

SERVES 8
**(if stirred into a soup)
8 garlic cloves, peeled
at least 24 fresh basil leaves
225g/8oz Parmesan cheese, freshly grated
150ml/5fl oz extra virgin olive oil**

Put the garlic in a food processor and process until finely chopped. Add the basil leaves and process until finely chopped, then add the grated Parmesan cheese and process again.

With the motor running, add the olive oil in a slow, steady stream through the feed tube until a thick green mayonnaise forms. Transfer to a bowl and use at once or cover the *pistou* with film to prevent air discolouring it and chill until required.

SALADE NIÇOISE

There are as many arguments about what constitutes a vraie salade Niçoise *as there are about* bouillabaisse. *Tuna is now an almost universal ingredient: originally it would have been too expensive. (Illustrated opposite)*

SERVES 4
**100g/ 3 ½ oz French-style green beans, topped and tailed
1 garlic clove, halved
4tbsp olive oil
4-6 basil leaves, shredded
1 small, round loose-leaf lettuce, leaves separated and well rinsed
200g/7oz tinned tuna, drained and flaked
1 green pepper, cored, seeded and cut into strips
4-6 very ripe tomatoes, quartered
2-3 hardboiled eggs, shelled
85g/3oz small black Niçois olives
12 anchovy fillets, cut into strips
salt and freshly ground black pepper**

Bring a saucepan of water to the boil. Place the green beans in a steamer on top and steam for about 5 minutes until just tender crisp. Put the beans in cold water to refresh, then drain. Leave until completely cool.

Meanwhile, rub a shallow salad bowl with the cut halves of garlic.

Mix the olive oil, basil and salt and pepper together in a bowl to make a dressing. Dry the lettuce leaves and toss them in a little of the dressing to coat, then use to line a salad bowl.

Put the tuna in the centre of the bowl and surround it with the beans and pepper. Arrange the tomatoes and hard-boiled eggs attractively in the bowl. Top with the olives and anchovies. Pour over the rest of the dressing. Do not toss. Serve immediately.

ASPERGES AU GRATIN

Asparagus au Gratin

This is a typical Provençal treatment of vegetables, which are briefly cooked as simply as possible and then 'sauced' with breadcrumbs and cheese, all designed to make a little go a lot further. You can use use white or green asparagus. I use white, which tends to benefit from longer cooking, but also because I think green asparagus superior and deserving of only the best treatment: simply steamed and served with hollandaise sauce.

SERVES 4
1.5kg/3 ¹/₂ lb asparagus, woody ends of stalks trimmed off and tied into 4 bundles
75g/2 ¹/₂ oz butter
55g/2oz Parmesan cheese, grated
100g/3 ¹/₂ oz Gruyère cheese, grated
55g/2oz fresh breadcrumbs
salt and freshly ground black pepper

Bring a wide sauté pan or frying pan of salted water to the boil. Gently drop in the asparagus bundles and return the water to the boil, then lower the heat slightly and cook the asparagus at a brisk simmer for 10-15 minutes until the stalks are tender when you pierce them with a knife. Alternatively, if you are using an asparagus steamer, place the bundles upright with the tips pointing upwards and steam for about 10 minutes.

When the asparagus bundles are cooked, drain and untie them, refresh under cold water and drain once again. Pat dry on a clean cloth.

Meanwhile, preheat the grill to medium and butter an oblong flameproof gratin dish long enough to hold the asparagus spears. Melt 45g/1 ¹/₂ oz of the butter and cut the remainder of it into small dice.

Make one layer of asparagus in the dish. Sprinkle with some of both cheeses and some melted butter. Place another layer of asparagus on top, head to toe with the layer below, and sprinkle with more cheese and butter. Season. Continue the layering and finish with cheese.

Top with the breadcrumbs and dot with the diced butter. Grill for about 3 minutes or until the top is nicely browned and the dish is heated through. Serve immediately.

TOMATES FARCIES 'GRAND-MERE MICHEL'

Stuffed Tomatoes

This dish was traditionally used as a way of making meat go further.

SERVES 4
8 large, firm tomatoes
8tbsp long-grain rice
150ml/5fl oz extra virgin olive oil
150g/5oz boned shoulder of pork, finely chopped
75g/2 ¹/₂ oz veal fillet, finely chopped
100g/3 ¹/₂ oz bacon fat, finely chopped
sprig flat-leaf parsley, finely chopped
sprig of tarragon, finely chopped
sprig of basil, finely chopped
sprig of thyme, finely chopped
1 bay leaf, finely chopped
1 onion, finely chopped
1 garlic clove, finely chopped
salt and freshly ground black pepper

Preheat the oven to 180°C/350°F/gas mark 4. Cut the top off each tomato to make a lid about 2.5cm/1in thick. Put the lids to one side.

Use a spoon to scoop all the juice and seeds from the tomatoes into a sieve set over a bowl.

Then, being careful not to break the skins, scoop as much of the flesh from the tomatoes as you can into another bowl. Mash to a pulp.

Put the tomato shells inside a gratin dish so they fit tightly together and season the insides with salt and freshly ground black pepper. Add 1 tablespoon of the rice to each tomato shell and pour in a little of the tomato juice and olive oil, then set aside.

Add all the chopped meats, the herbs and the onion and garlic to the bowl with the tomato pulp, stir together well and season.

Spoon the mixture into the tomato shells without packing it in too much but piling it into a dome on top. Place the tomato lids on top, then sprinkle with any remaining tomato juice and the rest of the olive oil.

Put in the oven and cook for 40-45 minutes until the lids are well browned and wrinkled.

PISSALADIERE

Onion Tart

This onion and anchovy tart is Nice's version of the Italian pizza. It should have a thin, crisp base and a thick topping of thinly sliced onion. A proper one is topped with pissala, *a strong fish paste made from the small fry of sardines and anchovies. But this is increasingly rare and, even in Nice, anchovy fillets are generally substituted. (Illustrated opposite)*

SERVES 1, OR 4 AS A LIGHT SNACK
FOR THE DOUGH
8g/ ¹/₄ oz live yeast
125ml/4fl oz warm water
225g/ ¹/₂ lb strong bread flour plus extra for rolling out dough
15g/ ¹/₂ oz sugar
8g/ ¹/₄ oz salt

FOR THE FILLING
150ml/5fl oz olive oil, plus extra
for sprinkling
1.5kg/3 ½ lb onions, thinly sliced
2 garlic cloves, crushed
bouquet garni consisting of 1 sprig of
thyme, 1 bay leaf and 1 sprig of fennel
10 anchovy fillets, canned and drained
20 black olives, such as Niçois, unpitted

For the dough, mix the yeast with the warm water in a small bowl. Put the flour, sugar and salt into a large bowl and make a well in the centre. Pour the yeast mixture into the well. Using your hands, mix the dry ingredients gradually into the liquid until they form a smooth dough. Knead the dough, then cover with a damp cloth and leave to rise in a warm place for 1-1 ½ hours, until doubled in bulk.

Meanwhile, heat 1 tablespoon of the olive oil in a large saucepan over a low heat. Add the onions, garlic and bouquet garni and cook for about 10 minutes until the onions are very soft but not coloured, stirring carefully so that the onions and garlic do not burn.

Preheat the oven to 220°C/425°F/Gas 7.

Knock back the bread dough and roll it out on a lightly floured surface into a 20cm/8in round. Carefully place on a lightly oiled baking sheet and turn up the edge evenly to make a rim all round. Leave the dough for 15 minutes to let it rise a little. Bake for 10 minutes, then remove from the oven.

Remove the bouquet garni from the onions, then spread the onions thickly over the dough. Arrange the anchovy fillets on top and dot with the olives. Sprinkle with the rest of the olive oil, return the tart to the oven and continue baking for 15-20 minutes or until the crust browns. You can serve the *pissaladière* hot, warm or at room temperature, as a snack or as a light lunch.

ABOVE *Slices of mouthwatering* Pissaladière *are sold by vendors on the streets of Nice.*

CAILLETTES

Pork Liver and Swiss
Chard Sausages

Traditionally, these are flat sausages wrapped in caul fat but Patrick Boscq at his restaurant in Grasse, otherwise a staunch upholder of tradition, prefers to cook caillettes *in a terrine. You will also find them called* gayettes *on some menus: whichever, they are one of the very few examples of Provençal charcuterie.*

SERVES 4
100g/3 ½ oz chicken livers, well trimmed
and any green spots removed
100g/3 ½ oz pork liver
3tbsp Marc de Provence or Cognac
100g/3 ½ oz pork fat, finely chopped
100g/3 ½ oz Swiss chard leaves or spinach
leaves, coarsely shredded
1 large onion, finely chopped
3 garlic cloves, crushed
salt and freshly ground black pepper

Put the chicken and pork livers in a bowl, spoon over the Marc de Provence or Cognac and leave the livers to marinate overnight in a cool place.

Preheat the oven to 180°C/350°F/gas mark 4.

Remove the livers from the marinade and finely chop, then place in a large bowl with the remaining ingredients and mix together until well blended. Season well with salt and black pepper. Pack the mixture into a 1.5l/2 ½ pint terrine or mould, and cover.

Line a deep ovenproof dish with newspaper, then add the terrine. Pour in enough water to come half-way up the sides of the terrine. Put the dish in the oven and cook for at least 1 hour or until the *caillette* starts to come away from the sides of the terrine.

Remove from the oven and take the terrine out of the ovenproof dish. Uncover, place a double layer of foil on top of the *caillette* and a heavy weight on top of that (tins of food are fine). Leave to stand for at least 2 hours, or until cool. Chill until ready to serve, then unmould and slice.

PASTIS DE MOULES

Mussels in Pastis-flavoured Broth

Mussels are harvested from the rocky coastlines of Provence to make this aromatic seafood dish. This is similar to moules marinières *but the addition of* pastis *gives an aniseed flavour to the broth. Serve with fresh, crusty bread. (Illustrated below)*

SERVES 4

**2kg/2 ½ lb mussels, cleaned and with
beards removed
300ml/10fl oz dry white wine, such as
Sauvignon
100ml/3 ½ fl oz *pastis***

**3 shallots, finely chopped
4 garlic cloves, crushed
2tbsp olive oil
3 ripe tomatoes, peeled, seeded and chopped
1tbsp coriander seeds**

Discard any mussels that remain closed when you tap them sharply, or any that are damaged.

Put the wine, *pastis*, shallots, garlic, olive oil and tomatoes in a saucepan large enough to hold all the mussels and bring to the boil. Boil, uncovered, until the liquid is reduced by half.

Add the mussels and the coriander seeds, cover the pan and cook over a medium-high heat for 7-8 minutes until all the mussels open. Discard any mussels that remain closed.

Serve the mussels with the broth.

ECREVISSES A LA PROVENCALE

Crayfish, Provençal Style

A la provençale *denotes the presence of garlic and tomatoes, although until tomatoes became such an ubiquitous part of the cuisine a mere hundred or so years ago, it meant simply 'with garlic'. You can substitute* langoustines *for* crayfish, *if you wish.*

SERVES 4

**3tbsp olive oil
1 onion, finely chopped
1 carrot, diced
1kg/2 ¼ lb crayfish, cooked and shelled, tail
shells reserved
5tbsp Cognac
150ml/5fl oz dry white wine
2tbsp tomato purée
bouquet garni consisting of 1 sprig of
thyme, 1 bay leaf and 1 sprig of fennel
1 garlic clove, finely chopped
3-4 sprigs flat-leaf parsley, finely chopped
salt and freshly ground black pepper**

Heat the oil in a sauté pan or frying pan over a medium heat. Add the onion and carrot and cook, stirring occasionally, until lightly brown. Increase the heat, add the crayfish tail shells and stir-fry for 1 minute. Pour over the Cognac, set alight and flambé until the flames die down.

Stir in the wine and tomato purée and add the bouquet garni. Season well, then lower the heat and simmer, uncovered, for 5 minutes. Add the crayfish and toss for 2 minutes.

To serve, remove the bouquet garni and sprinkle over the garlic and parsley. Transfer to one large serving dish or 4 deep soup plates. Serve immediately.

SARDINES A LA PROVENCALE

Sardines, Provençal-style

SERVES 4

6tbsp olive oil

1 small red pepper, cored, seeded and thinly sliced

1 small green pepper, cored, seeded and thinly sliced

1 onion, finely chopped

2 ripe tomatoes, peeled and seeded

200ml/7fl oz dry white wine, such as Chardonnay

1tbsp tomato purée

bouquet garni consisting of 1 sprig of thyme, 1 bay leaf and 1 sprig of fennel

2 garlic cloves, finely chopped

16 fresh sardines, scaled and cleaned with heads removed

salt and freshly ground black pepper

Heat 3 tablespoons of the olive oil in a saucepan, then lower the heat, add the peppers and onion and cover and cook until the peppers are tender and the onion is translucent, stirring occasionally to make sure that the vegetables do not brown or burn. Add the tomatoes, wine and tomato purée and stir until well blended together, then add the bouquet garni and garlic. Simmer, uncovered, over a low heat for about 20 minutes.

Meanwhile, rinse the sardines inside and out, then pat very dry with paper towels. Season well with salt and pepper. Heat the remaining olive oil in two separate frying pans. Add half the sardines to each pan and quickly sear on both sides. Remove the bouquet garni and pour half the sauce into each pan, lower the heat and simmer for 5 minutes. Serve the sardines immediately.

SARDINES FARCIES

Stuffed Sardines
(Illustrated above)

SERVES 4

1kg/2¼ lb fresh spinach, stalks removed

2tbsp olive oil plus extra for brushing

1 onion, finely chopped

1tbsp flour

3tbsp milk, warmed

½ tsp grated nutmeg

2 garlic cloves, finely chopped

24 small, fresh sardines, scaled and gutted with heads removed

55g/2oz dry breadcrumbs

salt and freshly ground black pepper

Bring a large saucepan of lightly salted water to the boil, then add the spinach and simmer for 5 minutes. Drain, refresh under cold water, drain again and squeeze out all the excess moisture. Finely chop the spinach.

Preheat the oven to 230°C/450°F/gas mark 8 and heavily grease a baking tray with olive oil.

Heat the oil in a saucepan, then lower the heat, add the onion and cover and cook until it is translucent. Do not let it brown. Stir in the flour and the spinach, and cook for about 2 minutes until it thickens. Stir in the warm milk and season with nutmeg, salt and pepper. Cook the sauce for 2-3 minutes over a medium heat, stirring constantly until it thickens and the flour doesn't taste raw. Stir in the garlic and remove the pan from the heat.

Rinse the sardines inside and out, then pat them very dry. Place each fish flesh side downwards, and flattten by pressing your hand on the backbone. Turn the fish over and season with salt, then place 1-2 tablespoons of filling on 12 sardines. Top with the remaining fish, flesh side down to make a sandwich.

Put each pair of fish on the baking tray. Brush with oil and sprinkle with breadcrumbs. Cook for 10 minutes until the fish are browned and the flesh flakes if tested with a knife.

PINTADE AUX OLIVES

Guinea Fowl with Olives

*This dish would originally have been made
with song birds or, at the very least, pigeons.
You can also use pheasant for a more gamy
dish. Do not be tempted to add the olives any
sooner than specified: if they are cooked for a
long time they will impart bitterness to the
sauce. (Illustrated above)*

SERVES 4
4tbsp olive oil
**1 guinea fowl weighing 1.5kg/3½lb, cleaned
and cut into 8 pieces**

100g/3½oz pork belly, finely diced
1 onion, finely chopped
**200ml/7fl oz dry white wine,
such as Chardonnay**
200ml/7fl oz chicken stock
1tbsp plain flour
**bouquet garni consisting of 1 sprig of
thyme, 1 bay leaf and 1 sprig of fennel**
24 green olives, rinsed, stoned and halved
salt and freshly ground black pepper

Heat 2 tablespoons of the olive oil in a flameproof casserole. Add the guinea fowl pieces
in batches and sauté until they are browned.
Remove from the casserole and keep warm.

Add the remaining olive oil to the
casserole. When it is hot, add the pork pieces
and onion and cook, stirring occasionally, until
they start to brown, then stir in the white wine
and continue cooking until it is reduced by
half. Add the stock and flour and simmer until
the sauce thickens slightly.

Return the guinea fowl to the casserole and
add the bouquet garni. Cover tightly and
simmer for 45 minutes, turning the bird pieces
several times. Add extra water if necessary.

Transfer the guinea fowl to a warmed
serving platter and keep warm. De-grease the
cooking liquid in the casserole, then pour it
through a conical sieve into a clean pan. Add
the olives and heat through, then season. Pour
the sauce over the guinea fowl and serve.

LOU FASSUM

Stuffed Cabbage

Patrick Boscq, chef/patron of Maître Boscq in Grasse, is the self-proclaimed 'king of stuffed cabbage'. Ideally, he would cook the cabbage for at least eight hours, but says three is sufficient. M. Boscq suggests using a clean hairnet to cook the cabbage in, but a piece of muslin is a far more realistic option. The maître *also points out that this is a modern version of the original recipe: it would have been very unusual for it to have contained meat. To help the cabbage keep its shape after cooking, remove it to a colander to drain and then transfer it to a deep dish. The stock is served separately as a soup. (Illustrated right)*

SERVES 6-8

1 large open-hearted cabbage, such as Savoy
285g/10oz belly of pork, finely chopped
285g/10oz beef chuck, finely chopped
125g/4 ¹/₂ oz tinned petits pois
285g/10oz green Swiss chard leaves, finely sliced
100g/3 ¹/₂ oz long-grain rice
2 onions, finely chopped
1tbsp fresh sage, finely chopped
3 garlic cloves, finely chopped
2 eggs, lightly beaten
1.5l/2 ¹/₂ pt chicken or vegetable stock
salt and freshly ground black pepper

Put the whole cabbage in large saucepan or stockpot, cover with cold water and bring to the boil. Drain immediately, refresh under cold water and drain again.

Separate the cabbage leaves and finely slice the cabbage heart. Place the sliced heart in a large bowl with the remaining ingredients and mix together until well blended. Season well.

Line a large salad bowl with a piece of muslin, then line it with several layers of the largest cabbage leaves. Place the stuffing mixture between the leaves as well as in the centre, then pull up the edges of the muslin and tie securely with kitchen string to make a neat, compact ball.

Put the stock into the rinsed-out saucepan or stockpot and bring to the boil, then lower the heat, add the cabbage, cover the pan and cook very slowly over the lowest possible heat for at least 3 hours, topping up the water if necessary.

To serve, use a fork to lift the cabbage by the net out of the pan and drain it in a colander. Place the cabbage ball on a large, deep platter and cut into wedges. Serve the stock as a soup on the side.

GRAS-DOUBLE A LA PROVENCALE

Tripe, Provençal Style

Tripe is still popular all over Provence, although it is rarely cooked at home. Either it is bought ready-made or enthusiasts know when the local restaurant serves it as the plat du jour.

SERVES 4

1kg/2 ¹/₄ lb ox tripe
15g/ ¹/₂ oz lard
100g/3 ¹/₂ oz pork belly, diced
2 onions, chopped
4 tomatoes, chopped
500ml/16fl oz dry white wine, heated
bouquet garni consisting of 1 sprig of thyme, 1 bay leaf, 1 sprig of parsley and a piece of celery stalk
2 garlic cloves, finely chopped
2-3 sprigs flat-leaf parsley, finely chopped
salt and freshly ground black pepper

Put the tripe in a large saucepan of cold water over a high heat and bring to the boil, then blanch for 10 minutes. Drain well and leave to cool, then cut into 5x1cm/2x ¹/₂ in strips. Season well and set aside.

Preheat the oven to 150°C/300°F/gas mark 2.

Melt the lard in a large flameproof casserole over a medium heat. Add the pork belly and cook, stirring occasionally, until browned on all sides. Add the onion and continue cooking it until it lightly browns. Stir in the tomatoes and cook for 5 minutes, stirring occasionally.

Stir in the wine, the bouquet garni and the tripe. Bring to the simmer, then cover and cook for 8 hours. Check occasionally and top up with water as necessary.

To serve, remove the bouquet garni and sprinkle with the garlic and parsley.

NOUGAT GLACE AU COULIS DE FRAMBOISE

Nougat Ice-Cream with Raspberry Sauce

Virtually every good restaurant in Provence offers this ice-cream whether it is made on the premises or shop-bought. As this is a fairly complicated ice-cream to make, you need specialist equipment, such as a copper sugar pan and a sugar thermometer to ensure complete success. Nevertheless, nothing beats the taste of home-made ice-cream. The raspberry sauce makes a refreshingly tart accompaniment. (Illustrated opposite)

SERVES 10
100ml/3 ½ fl oz rum
100g/3 ½ oz mixed crystallized fruit, such as pineapples, apricots, clementines, figs and orange zest, finely diced
550ml/18fl oz whipping cream
sprigs of mint, slices of kiwi fruit and extra whole raspberries, to decorate

FOR THE NOUGATINE
300g/10 ½ oz almonds
300g/10 ½ oz caster sugar

FOR THE ITALIAN MERINGUE
115g/4oz caster sugar
3 egg whites

FOR THE RASPBERRY COULIS
400g/14oz raspberries
45g/1 ½ oz caster sugar

Put the rum in a bowl and add the diced crystallized fruit. Leave to marinate for 2-3 hours, then remove the fruit and leave it to drain for 1 hour.

Meanwhile, make the nougatine. Preheat the oven to 250°C/475°F/gas mark 9. Put the almonds on an ungreased baking tray and put in the oven to toast for 3-4 minutes until the skins start to peel off and the nuts colour slightly. Transfer the nuts to a clean tea-towel, tie the ends together and rub off the skins. Lightly grease a marble slab or baking tray.

Use a copper sugar pan or a heavy-based saucepan to make a caramel in. Put the sugar in the pan with 125ml/4fl oz of water and stir to dissolve the sugar, then heat until the syrup becomes golden and reaches 115°C/240°F on a sugar thermometer. Pour in the almonds and immediately remove the pan from the heat. Use a long-handled wooden spoon to stir until all the almonds are completely covered in caramel. Pour them out on to the greased marble slab or baking tray and spread them out as thinly as possible into an even layer and leave until set and brittle.

Break the nougatine up into small pieces, put in a plastic bag and put in the freezer until next required.

To make the Italian meringue, put the caster sugar and 2 tablespoons of water in the rinsed-out copper sugar pan or a small, heavy-based saucepan, over a medium-high heat. Bring to the boil, stirring occasionally until the sugar dissolves. Use a wet pastry brush to wash the sugar crystals off the sides of the pan. Raise the heat to high and continue boiling, without stirring, until the mixture reaches 121°C/250°F on a sugar thermometer.

Meanwhile, use an electric mixer to beat the egg whites until stiff peaks form. Set the mixer to its lowest setting and slowly pour in the hot sugar syrup, making sure the syrup does not hit the beaters. Continue mixing until the mixture is cool, then chill until required.

Pour the whipping cream into a bowl and whisk until it begins to thicken. Stir in the cool

Italian meringue, the frozen nougatine and the drained fruit. Put the mixture into individual freezerproof moulds or a rectangular terrine and freeze for at least 4 hours until the mixture is of solid ice-cream consistency.

Meanwhile, make the raspberry *coulis*. Put the raspberries and sugar in a pan over a high heat and stir until the sugar dissolves. Bring to the boil, then lower the heat and simmer for 2 minutes. Using a wooden spoon, press the berries through a fine nylon sieve into a bowl. Leave to cool, then cover with film and chill.

To serve, unmould the individual desserts or the large terrine by rubbing a kitchen cloth soaked in hot water all over the base and sides. Invert carefully on to individual plates or a large plate. If you have made one large terrine, slice it up and arrange the slices on individual plates. Spoon the raspberry *coulis* around and decorate with a few sprigs of fresh mint, kiwi fruit slices and extra raspberries. Serve immediately.

A VISITOR'S GUIDE

This guide is a selection of restaurants, food shops, vineyards, markets and other places of interest, drawn from among the many hundreds I have visited over more than a decade.

All the restaurants listed cover a relatively wide price range. The prices are à la carte and include food only. Good Côtes de Provence wines will cost from 150FF to 200FF, top *appellations*, such as Châteauneuf-du-Pape will cost up to 500FF, depending on the vintage. There will always be a modest *vin du pays* at a corresponding price, available either by the carafe or by the bottle.

It is worth bearing in mind that most restaurants have extremely good value

menus du jour, and that even the most expensive will offer a reasonably priced fixed lunch menu on weekdays.

Having said that, it is easy to find indifferent food, especially in the tourist areas. Beware those menus that are printed and laminated; the dishes will not be responding to seasons or market availability.

Spring and autumn are the best times to find the widest range of good value food. Prices tend to be hiked up during the summer tourist season and many of the restaurants close from December to Easter. Even those who stay open will often close for a week or two in February when the French schools are on holiday.

Shops still close for lunch, usually between 12.30 and 2.30pm, but they are open until about 7.30 or 8.00pm. Most olive mills have shops attached which are open year-round, but the mills themselves will only be in action from September to February during the harvest.

Dégustation signs to vineyards abound and, even if the tasting room looks disappointingly closed, there's usually someone around to respond to the bell you're invited to ring. The only times visitors may not be welcomed is in autumn during the harvest, when all hands are busy picking. There are also larger wine co-operatives all over Provence which are

open six or seven days a week. If you're self-catering it is worth investing a few francs in a refillable five-litre container (a 'cubi').

Many restaurants and shops are closed all day Monday and national museums and art galleries are closed on Tuesdays. Even quite small villages have a *syndicat d'initiative* (larger towns will have an *office du tourisme*) which can supply maps and leaflets on local events. They will also have a list of local holidays and fêtes.

Key to symbols used in this Guide:
- ••• 300FF or more per person
- •• About 250FF per person
- • Up to 200FF per person

BOUCHES-DU-RHONE

Restaurants

L'ESCALE •••
promenade du Port
13620 Carry-le-Rouet
Tel 42 45 00 47 (page 31)

LA REGALIDO •••
rue Frédéric-Mistral
13990 Fontvieille
Tel 90 54 60 22

LE CLOS DE LA VIOLETTE •••
10 avenue de la Violette
13100 Aix-en-Provence
Tel 42 23 30 71

LES FRERES LANI ••
22 rue Leydet
13100 Aix-en-Provence
Tel 42 27 76 16

LE BISTRO LATIN ••
18 rue Couronne, 13100 Aix-en-Provence
Tel 42 38 22 88

LOU MARQUES •••
9 boulevard des Lices, 13631 Arles
Tel 90 93 43 20

LE VACCARES •••
place du Forum, 13200 Arles
Tel 90 96 06 17 (page 32)

CHEZ GILBERT ••
19 quai des Baux, 13260 Cassis
Tel 42 01 71 36

L'OUSTAU DE BEAUMANIERE •••
Val d'Enfer
13520 Les-Baux, Tel 90 54 33 07

LA CABRO D'OR •••
Val d'Enfer
13520 Les-Baux
Tel 90 54 33 21

LA RIBOTO DE TAVEN •••
Val d'Enfer
13520 Les-Baux, Tel 90 54 34 23

CHEZ FONFON ••
138 Vallon-des-Auffes
13007 Marseille
Tel 91 52 14 38

LE BISTRO DU PARADOU ••
avenue de la Vallée-des-Baux
13125 Le Paradou
Tel 90 97 32 70

LE RELAIS SAINTE-VICTOIRE ••
chemin Plaine
13100 Beaurecueil
Tel 42 66 94 98

VALLON DE VALRUGUES •••
chemin Canto Cigalo
13210 Saint-Rémy-de-Provence
Tel 90 92 04 40

L'OUSTALET MAIANEN •
13910 Maillane
Tel 90 95 74 60

OU RAVI PROVENCAU ••
34 avenue Vallée-des-Baux
13520 Mausanne-les-Alpilles
Tel 90 54 31 11

L'ETAPE LANI ••
(off D6, Gardanne exit)
13320 Bouc-Bel-Air
Tel 42 22 61 90

LE CHALUT •
place Jean-Fasciola
13500 Carro, Tel 42 80 70 61

Places of interest

LA PETITE PROVENCE DU PARADOU
(miniature village)
75 avenue de la Vallée des Baux
13520 Le Paradou
Tel 90 54 35 75

MUSEE DES AROMES DE PROVENCE
(perfume distillery and museum)
34 boulevard Mirabeau
13210 Saint-Rémy-de-Provence
Tel 90 92 48 70

MUSEE GROBET-LABADIE
(Provençal domestic life)
Maison Diamantée
2 rue de la Prison, 13002 Marseille
Tel 91 55 10 19

MUSEON ARLATEN
(Provençal history: created by
Frédéric Mistral)
rue de la République, 13200 Arles
Tel 90 96 08 23

MUSEE DU RIZ DE CAMARGUE
(rice museum)
Le Sambuc, 13200 Arles
Tel 90 97 20 29

MUSEE CAMARGUAIS
(Camargue history)
Mas du Pont de Rousty, 13200 Arles
Tel 90 97 10 82

Specialities of the region

G. MOYNE-BRESSAND
(chocolate *Clous de Nîmes*)
20 boulevard Victor Hugo
30000 Nîmes
Tel 66 67 35 12

CHATEAU FERRY LACOMBE
(wine)
route de Saint-Maximin
13530 Trets-en-Provence
Tel 42 29 33 69

MOULIN DE BEDARRIDES
(olive oil)
13990 Fontvieille
Tel 90 54 70 04

CO-OPERATIVE OLEICOLE DE LA
VALLEE DES BAUX
(olives and olive oil)
Moulin J-M Cornille
rue Charloun Rieu
13520 Mausanne-les-Alpilles
Tel 90 54 32 37

*LEFT Marseille claims to be France's
oldest city. Today it is the capital
of Provence and France's
second largest town. Much of
Marseille is an urban sprawl, but
the old port retains its charm and
the lively fish market along the Quai
des Belges is well worth visiting.
BELOW Less than 30 kilometres
north of Marseille is the graceful
town of Aix-en-Provence.
The Cours Mirabeau is a tree-
shaded boulevard, lined with cafes.*

*LEFT The stark ruins of
Les Baux-de-Provence seem to rise
organically from their rocky
Alpille pinnacle. One of the most
famous sights in Provence,
Les Baux was the great medieval
centre of courtly love and
troubadours but was destroyed by
Cardinal Richelieu in the
seventeenth century. In the last
century, bauxite (taking its name
from the town) was discovered here.*

LES DELICES DE L'OLIVIER
(olives and olive products)
13990 Fontvieille
Tel 90 54 74 30

CHARCUTERIE MOUSSET
(*saucisson d'Arles*)
3 avenue de la République
13310 Saint Martin de Crau
Tel 90 47 30 40

LES CALISSONS DU ROY RENE
(*calissons*)
7 rue Papassaudi
13100 Aix-en-Provence
Tel 42 26 67 86

GENIN
(*saucisson d'Arles*)
rue des Porcelets
13200 Arles

MAISON LILAMAND & FILS
(crystallized fruits)
route d'Avignon
13210 Saint-Rémy-de-Provence
Tel 90 92 11 08

MAS DE LA DAME
(wine, olives and olive oil)
route D, 13520 Les-Baux-de-Provence
Tel 90 54 32 24

DOMAINE DE JARRAS
(Listel wine)
30220 Aigues-Mortes
Tel 66 53 63 65

CLOS SAINTE-MAGDELEINE
(wine)
avenue de Revestel, 13260 Cassis
Tel 42 01 70 28

DOMAINE DU PATERNEL
(wine)
chemin des Janots
13260 Cassis
Tel 42 01 76 50

CHATEAU SIMONE
(Palette wine)
13590 Meyreuil
Tel 42 28 92 58

Markets

Daily: *Aix* (*not* Wednesday)
Sunday: *Martigues*
Monday: *Fontvieille*
Wednesday: *Arles, Saint Rémy, Salon-
  de-Provence*
Friday: *Cassis*
Saturday: *Arles*

Fêtes

January: *wine*, Saint-Vincent,
  Coudoux
February: *parade of the Black Virgin*,
  Marseille
Whitsun: *flower fair*, Tarascon
April: *cowboys*, Camargue
May: *gypsy fair*, Saintes-Maries-
  de-la-Mer
June: *garlic and terracotta*, Marseille;
  water dragon fair, Tarascon
July: *garlic fair*, Cabriés
August: *festival of Saint-Louis*
  (*medieval pageants*), Aigues-Mortes
September: *rice*, Arles; *wine*, Nîmes
October: *salt and wine*, Aigues-
  Mortes; *blessing of the sea*, Saintes-
  Maries-de-la-Mer
November: *wine and food*, Martigues
December: *santons*, Arles

VAUCLUSE

Restaurants

RESTAURANT PIC ●●●
285 avenue Victor Hugo
26000 Valence
Tel 75 44 15 32

LE PRIEURE ●●●
7 place du Chapitre
30400 Villeneuve-les-Avignon
Tel 90 25 18 20

LA BEAUGRAVIERE ●●
route Nationale 7
84430 Mondragon
Tel 90 40 82 54

HIELY-LUCULLUS ●●
5 rue de la République
84000 Avignon
Tel 90 85 17 07

CHRISTIAN ETIENNE ●●●
10-12 rue Mons, 84000 Avignon
Tel 90 86 16 50

CAFE DES ARTISTES ●
place Crillon, 84000 Avignon
Tel 90 82 63 16

HOSTELLERIE DE
CRILLON-LE-BRAVE ●●
place Eglise, 84410 Crillon-le-Brave
Tel 90 65 61 61 (page 56)

LE VERT-GALANT ●
12 rue Clapies
84200 Carpentras
Tel 90 67 15 50

LA SAULE PLEUREUR ●●●
quartier Beauregard, 84170 Monteux
Tel 90 62 01 35

LA PREVOTE ●
4 rue J-J. Rousseau
84800 L'Isle-sur-la-Sorgue
Tel 90 38 57 29

ALAIN NICOLET ●●
route de Pertuis
84460 Cheval-Blanc
Tel 90 78 01 56

BERNARD MATHYS ●●●
84400 la Chêne
Tel 90 04 84 64

AUBERGE DE LA LOUBE ●
84480 Bouox
Tel 90 74 19 58

LA FENIERE ●●
9 rue Grand-Pré, 84160 Lourmarin
Tel 90 68 11 79

Places of interest

UNIVERSITE DU VIN
(wine courses)
Le Château
26790 Suze-la-Rousse
Tel 75 04 86 09

MAISON DE LA TRUFFE
(truffle museum)
rue de la République
26130 Saint-Paul-Trois-Château
Tel 75 96 61 29

TOP *Fruity olive oils have become favourites of France's chefs. Extra virgin oils are still being pressed in the traditional way in mills such as this one in Nyons.*
ABOVE *The best of Provence's wines come from the Côtes-du-Rhône where the red wines of Gigondas rival those of Châteauneuf-du-Pape.*
RIGHT *The best of the almond harvest is combined to make deliciously sweet white and black nougat.*

MUSEE DE L'OLIVIER
place Olivier-de-Serres, 26110 Nyons
Tel 75 26 19 98

MUSEE DE LA BOULANGERIE
12 rue de la République
84480 Bonnieux
Tel 90 75 88 34

VILLAGE DES BORIES
(reconstructed 17th-century village)
84220 Gordes
Tel 90 72 03 48

Specialities of the region

CHATEAU DE SAINT-COSME
(wine)
84190 Gigondas
Tel 90 65 86 97 (page 55)

AUGIER & FILS
(honey)
84110 Vaison-la-Romaine
Tel 90 46 46 46 (page 49)

LA SCOURTINERIE
(woven hemp mats)
36 la Maladrerie, 26110 Nyons
Tel 75 26 33 52 (pages 48, 49)

J. RAMADE
(olives and olive oil)
7 impasse du Moulin, 26110 Nyons
Tel 75 26 08 18

CO-OPERATIVE AGRICOLE DU
NYONSAIS
(olives and olive oil)
place Olivier-de-Serres
26110 Nyons
Tel 75 26 03 44 (page 48)

MOULIN DU PONT ROMAN
(olives and olive oil)
4 promenade de la Digue, 26110 Nyons
Tel 75 26 11 00 (page 48)

MANGUIN
(*eaux-de-vie*)
Ile de la Barthelasse, 84000 Avignon
Tel 90 82 62 29 (page 48)

L'ABBAYE DE NOTRE DAME
(liqueurs)
Distillerie d'Aiguebelle
Montjoyer, 26230 Grignan
Tel 75 98 51 22 (page 53)

MONASTERE SAINTE-MADELEINE
(bread)
84339 Le Barroux
Tel 90 62 56 31

JOUVAUD
(crystallized fruits)
rue de l'Evêché, 84200 Carpentras
Tel 90 63 15 38

CHABERT ET GUILLOT
(nougat)
1 rue André-Ducatez
26200 Montélimar
Tel 75 01 47 22

AUX TROIS PETITS COCHONS
(*charcuterie*)
5 rue Stassart, 84100 Orange
Tel 90 34 63 58

PLANTIN
(truffles)
Le Saffre Puyméras
84110 Vaison-la-Romaine
Tel 90 46 41 44

MARIUS DUMAS (bread)
Porte d'Amont, 84260 Sarrians
Tel 90 65 42 15

LOU CANESTOU (cheese)
10 rue Raspail, 84110 Vaison-la-Romaine
Tel 90 36 31 30

JULIEN GREGOIRE (*herbes de Provence*)
84360 Mérindol
Tel 90 72 80 85

LES VINS DU TROUBADOUR (wine)
Cave des Vignerons, 84190 Vacqueyras
Tel 90 65 84 54

DOMAINE DE DURBAN (wine)
84190 Beaumes-de-Venise
Tel 90 62 94 26

Markets

Daily: *Avignon (not* Monday*)*
Sunday: *L'Isle-sur-la-Sorgue*
Monday: *Bollène, Cavaillon*
Tuesday: *Vaison-la-Romaine*
Wednesday: *Sault, Valréas*
Thursday: *Nyons, Orange*
Friday: *Carpentras*
Saturday: *Apt*

Fêtes

April: *wine*, Villeneuve-les-Avignon
Whitsun: *wine*, La Baume-de-Transit
June: *harvest*, Valréas
July: *wine*, Cairanne; *wine*,
    Carpentras; *wine*, Visan; *wine*,
    Vacqueras; *Picodon cheese*, Saou
August: *folklore and wine*, Séguret
November: *food and wine*,
    Vaison-la-Romaine

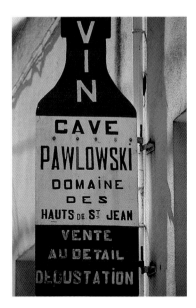

TOP RIGHT *Saint-Tropez is by far the most famous, and the most popular, of the many resorts of the Var.*
ABOVE AND TOP LEFT *Provence's reputation for producing mediocre wines is starting to be changed by enlightened wine makers such as Henri Pawlowski, near les Arcs, and the Matton family at Château Minuty, near Saint-Tropez*
LEFT *One of the abiding charms of Provence are the local markets like this one, held every Tuesday at Lorgues, near Draguignan.*

VAR

Restaurants

LA TABLE DU MARCHE ●●●
38 rue Clemenceau, 83990 Saint-Tropez
Tel 94 97 85 20 (page 78)

LA ROCHE AIGUILLE ●●
83111 Ampus, Tel 94 70 97 24

L'OUSTAOU ●
5 place Brémond, 83780 Flayosc
Tel 94 70 42 69

CHEZ BRUNO ●●
route de Vidauban, 83510 Lorgues
Tel 94 73 92 19

LE LOGIS DU GUETTEUR ●●
place du Château, 83460 Les Arcs
Tel 94 73 30 82

LE JARDIN DE PERLE-FLEURS ●●●
100 chemin de l'Orangerie
83230 Bormes-les-Mimosas
Tel 94 64 99 23

LE RELAIS DES ADRETS ●●●
place de la Mairie, 83600 Les Adrets
Tel 94 40 90 88

LE LINGOUSTO ●●●
route de Pierrefeu
83390 Cuers
Tel 94 28 69 10

LA VERDOYANTE ●●
866 chemin de Coste Brigade
83580 Gassin
Tel 94 56 16 23

LES ROCHES ●●●
1 avenue Trois-Dauphins
83980 Aiguebelle
Tel 94 71 05 05

AUBERGE DU FENOUILLET ●●
20 avenue General-de-Gaulle
83260 La Crau
Tel 94 66 76 74

LA GRILLADE AU FEU DE BOIS ●●
83340 Le Luc, Tel 94 69 71 20

Places of interest

CHATEAU DE VINS
(summer concerts, plays and
   exhibitions)
Château de Vins-sur-Caramy
83170 Brignoles
Tel 94 72 50 40

PALAIS DES COMTES DE PROVENCE
(traditional Provençal kitchen)
83170 Brignoles
Tel 94 69 45 18

CHATEAU D'ENTRECASTEAUX
(house and garden)
83570 Entrecasteaux
Tel 94 04 43 95

Specialities of the region

MAX RABEL
(chocolates, patisserie, ice-cream)
14 boulevard Georges Clemenceau
83300 Draguignan
Tel 94 68 16 34

LES RUCHERS DU BESSILLON
(honey)
2 rue des Naïs, 83850 Cotignac
Tel 94 04 60 39

MICKA (tarte Tropézienne)
9 rue Louis-Leblanc
83990 Saint-Tropez

SENEQUIER (nougat)
4 place aux Herbes
83990 Saint-Tropéz
Tel 94 97 00 90

LA MAISON DES VINS COTES DE
PROVENCE
(wine tastings, shop and restaurant)
Route Nationale 7, 83460 Les Arcs
Tel 94 73 31 01

CHATEAU MINUTY (wine)
route de Ramatuelle, 83580 Gassin
Tel 94 56 12 09

DOMAINE DES FERAUD (wine)
83550 Vidauban
Tel 94 73 03 12

CHATEAU SAINTE-ROSELINE (wine)
83460 Les Arcs
Tel 94 73 32 57

DOMAINE LA BERNARDE (wine)
83340 Le Luc
Tel 94 60 71 31

DOMAINE DE L'ABBAYE (wine)
83340 le Thoronet
Tel 94 73 87 36

CHATEAU VIGNELAURE
route de Jouques, 83560 Rians
Tel 94 80 31 93

DOMAINE DES HAUTS DE
SAINT-JEAN (wine)
route Sainte-Roselyne
83460 Les Arcs
Tel 94 73 31 48

MAISON DES VINS DE BANDOL
(wine)
allée Vivien
83150 Bandol
Tel 94 29 45 03

Markets

Sunday: *Toulon*
Tuesday: *Lorgues, Roquebrune-
   sur-Argens*
Wednesday: *Aups, Brignoles,
   Draguignan*
Thursday: *Barjols, Fayence,
   Le Lavandou, Toulon*
Friday: *Flassans-sur-Issole,
   Roquebrune-sur-Argens*
Saturday: *Aups, Barjols, Brignoles,
   Draguignan, Fayence, Saint-Tropez,
   Toulon*

Fêtes

January: *tripe festival*, Barjols
April: *wine*, Brignoles
July: *olives*, Draguignan
August: *wine*, Vidauban;
   garlic, Hyères;
   folklore, Cogolin

RIGHT The river Verdon carves its way through the canyon of the Gorges du Verdon, forming a dramatic border between the Var and Alpes-de-Haute-Provence, before flowing into the more peaceful vista of Lac de Sainte-Croix.
FAR RIGHT Banon is typical of the hilltop villages of the Alpes-de-Haute-Provence; it is justly famous for its goats' cheese.

ALPES-DE-HAUTE-PROVENCE

Restaurants

LA BONNE ETAPE ●●●
chemin du Lac
04160 Chateaux-Arnoux
Tel 92 64 00 09 (page 97)

LE GRAND PARIS ●●
19 boulevard Thiers
04000 Digne
Tel 92 31 11 15

MA PETITE AUBERGE ●
N85 (route Napoléon)
04000 Digne
Tel 92 35 56 52

LA MANGEOIRE ●
place Quatre-Vents
04400 Barcelonnette
Tel 92 81 01 61

L'AVENUE ●
avenue Gare, 04240 Annot
Tel 92 83 22 07

AU FAISAN DORE ●
Route Nationale 96
04310 Peyruis
Tel 92 68 00 51

LE VIEUX COLOMBIER ●●
La Bastide-Blanche, 04190 Dabisse
Tel 92 34 32 32

HOSTELLERIE DE LA FUSTE ●●●
04210 La Fuste
Tel 92 72 92 93

LE BOIS D'ASSON ●●
D13 (route de Forcalquier)
04300 Saint-Maim
Tel 92 79 51 20

LA CREMAILLERE ●●
route de Riez, 04800 Groux-les-Bains
Tel 92 74 22 29

LES SANTONS ●●
place Eglise, 04360 Moustiers-Ste-Marie
Tel 92 74 66 48

NOUVEL HOTEL DU COMMERCE ●
place Eglise, 04120 Castellane
Tel 92 83 61 00

AUBERGE DU POINT SUBLIME ●
04120 Rougon, Tel 92 83 60 35

Specialities of the region

ATELIER DE SEGRIES
(handpainted *faïence* pottery)
04360 Moustiers-Sainte-Marie
Tel 92 74 66 69

CANTERPERDRIX
(nougat and *calissons*)
place de la République, 04200 Sisteron
Tel 92 61 08 41

Markets

Monday: *Forcalquier*
Tuesday: *Banon*
Wednesday: *Barcelonnette, Digne, Sisteron, Riez (truffles, Nov-March)*
Thursday: *Digne*
Friday: *Colmars-les-Alpes*
Saturday: *Barcelonnette, Beausoleil, Castellane, Digne, Manosque, Riez, Sisteron*

Fêtes

August: *folklore,* Forcalquier; *lavender,* Digne

ALPES MARITIMES

Restaurants

RESTAURANT DE BACON ●●●
boulevard Bacon
06600 Cap d'Antibes
Tel 93 61 50 02 (page 118)

LE RELAIS A MOUGINS ●●
place de la Mairie
06250 Mougins
Tel 93 90 03 47 (page 119)

LE MOULIN DE MOUGINS ●●●
424 chemin du Moulin
06250 Mougins
Tel 93 75 78 24

L'AMANDIER DE MOUGINS ●●●
place du Cdt-Lamy
06250 Mougins
Tel 93 90 00 91

BAR RENE SOCCA ●
2 rue Miralhétti, 06000 Nice
Tel 93 62 37 81

LA MERENDA ●
4 rue de la Terrasse
06000 Nice
(no telephone)

MAITRE BOSCQ ●
13 rue Fontelle, 06130 Grasse
Tel 93 36 45 76

AUBERGE NOSSI-BE ●
place Portail
06810 Auribeau-sur-Saigne
Tel 93 42 20 20

AUBERGE DU COLOMBIER ●
06330 Roquefort-les-Pins
Tel 93 77 10 27

LA PALME D'OR ●●●
73 Croisette
06400 Cannes
Tel 92 98 74 14

LE ROYAL GRAY ●●●
6 rue des Etats-Unis
06400 Cannes
Tel 92 99 79 79

LA GOUSSE D'AIL ●
11 avenue Grasse
06220 Vallauris
Tel 93 64 10 71

AUBERGE DE LA MADONE ●●
06440 Peillon
Tel 93 79 91 17

LA CHANDELLERIE ●
7 rue de la Mairie
06560 Valbonne
Tel 93 12 03 66

Places of interest

MUSEE DE L'ART CULINAIRE
(birthplace of Auguste Escoffier)
06270 Villeneuve-Loubet
Tel 93 20 80 51

MUSEE D'HISTOIRE LOCALE
(with 19th-century kitchen)
6 place de la Chapelle, 06410 Biot
Tel 93 65 11 79

ABOVE People-watching is always a popular pastime: here the crowds survey the scene from a cafe in Nice.

BELOW A tranquil scene at the Relais à Mougins, a restaurant in the picturesque village of Mougins.

PARFUMERIE FRAGONARD
(perfume)
20 boulevard Fragonard
06130 Grasse
Tel 93 36 44 65

Specialities of the region

CONFISERIE DES GORGES DU LOUP
(crystallized fruits)
Pont du Loup
06140 Tourettes-sur-Loup
Tel 93 59 32 91 (page 115)

CONFISERIE DU VIEUX NICE
(crystallized fruits)
14 quai Papcino
06300 Nice
Tel 93 55 43 50

LA VERRERIE DE BIOT
(glass and pottery)
chemin des Combes
06410 Biot
Tel 93 65 03 00

LA FERME SAVOYARDE
(cheese)
22 rue Meynadier
06400 Cannes
Tel 93 39 63 68

AU BON RAVIOLIS
(pasta)
31 rue Meynadier, 06400 Cannes
Tel 93 39 36 63

AU ROI DU CHAROLAIS
(roast suckling pig)
38 rue Meynadier
06400 Cannes
Tel 93 39 09 93

BRUNO
(confectionery)
50 rue d'Antibes
06400 Cannes
Tel 93 39 26 63

MAIFFRET
(confectionery)
31 rue d'Antibes
06400 Cannes
Tel 93 39 08 29

ESPUNO
(bread)
22 rue Vernier
06000 Nice
Tel 93 88 83 33

LE FOUR A BOIS
33 rue Droite
06300 Nice
Tel 93 80 50 67

HENRI AUER
(crystallized fruits)
7 rue St-François-de-Paule
06300 Nice
Tel 93 85 77 98

ALZIARI
(olives and olive oil)
14 rue Saint-François-de-Paule
06300 Nice
Tel 93 85 76 92

HUILERIE DE LA BRAGUE
(olives and olive oil)
2 route de Châteuneuf
06650 Opio
Tel 93 77 23 03

CO-OPERATIVE NEROLIUM
(orange and rose flower water)
12 avenue Clemenceau
06220 Vallauris, Tel 93 64 27 54

Markets

Daily: *Cannes, Nice (not* Monday*)*
Sunday: *Vallauris*
Tuesday: *Antibes*
Wednesday: *Grasse, Menton, Vallauris*
Thursday: *Antibes, Grasse, Menton,
    Mouans-Sartoux*
Friday: *Cagnes-sur-Mer, Grasse,
    Menton, Valbonne, Vence,
    Villefranche-sur-Mer*
Saturday: *Antibes, Grasse, Menton*

Fêtes

February: *lemons*, Menton
May: *roses*, Grasse; *cheese*, Cannes
August: *jasmin*, Grasse
September: *wine*, Biot; *folklore*, Peille
November: *chestnuts*, Isola

ABOVE AND LEFT *Grasse, perched
precariously on a hillside just
north of Cannes, is known as the
'balcony of the Côte'. Most
famous for its perfume industry
based on locally-grown
jasmine, roses and orange blossoms,
the town was developed during
the last century as a health
resort. Queen Victoria spent several
winters here. The streets, lined
with tall, medieval houses,
are cobbled, narrow and twisting
with almost every bend
revealing a worthwhile
'photo-opportunity'.*

LIST OF RECIPES

INDEX

PUBLISHER'S ACKNOWLEDGMENTS

The publisher would like to thank the photographers and organisations for their permission to reproduce the following photographs:

6-7 above right, Agence Top/M.J. Jarry/J.F. Tripelon; 8-9 below, Explorer/P. Brylac; 26 left, Michael Busselle; 27 above right, Explorer/Firadou; 28 below right, Explorer/Jalain; 68-9 Image Bank/Chris Thompson; 70-71 Images Colour Library; 74 above, Agence Top/Pierre Hussenot; 106 below, Jerrican/Zintzmeyer; 109 Barrie Smith; 110-111 above, Explorer/Donnezan; 116 Jerrican/Charron; 116 Agence Top/ Herve Champollion.

For the recipe photography (pages 35, 37, 38, 41, 43, 59, 63, 64-66, 80-83, 85, 86, 89, 98, 99, 101, 102, 105, 120, 124, 126, 129)

Home Economist	Jane Suthering
Assistant	Emma Patmore
Stylist	Roisin Nield
Assistant	Camilla Bambrough

Index	Karin Woodruff
Map	Clare Melinsky
Recipe Consultant	Linda Collister

AUTHOR'S ACKNOWLEDGMENTS

My thanks go to all the people mentioned in these pages who gave their help and their time over several months. I couldn't have written this book without them – and the research wouldn't have been as much fun.

At Conran Octopus, Sarah Pearce, Karen Bowen and Charlotte Coleman-Smith were indispensable in organizing my words into a coherent and attractive whole. Thanks also to Fiona Lindsay for making the introduction.

I am – as always – grateful for the friendship and generosity of Egon Ronay and Robyn and Michel Roux. In Provence, Micheline Turner gave much advice, sharing her great store of local knowledge, and Emma Hodder helped enormously with the research and translation.

Jane Suthering brought the recipes to life for photography and Debbie Patterson's photographs evoke the spirit of Provence.

Most of all, I thank John Hodder who gave up two months of his work – and his waistline — to drive more than six thousand kilometres with me, eating and cooking in all five *départements*, and then spent another six weeks helping me taste and test recipes back home in London.

PHOTOGRAPHER'S ACKNOWLEDGMENTS

With special thanks to Charm Eberle, Cassandre Lavoix and family in Sisteron; Jany Gleize at La Bonne Etape; all at Château de Saint-Cosme, Gigondas; BB in the Camargue; Sylvia Ellis in Villecroze and her friends Kate and Leonard, Serge Piro and his father; Henri Pawlowski, and last but not least, the 'Location Team', Jane Suthering and her assistant Emma, Karen and Ron Bowen; and 'Mission Control', Sarah Pearce and Charlotte Coleman-Smith.

Thanks also to: La Poterie du Soleil, Quartier Colombier, 83690 Villecroze, France; Souleiado, 171 Fulham Road, London SW3.